HILARIOUS M.B.A MEMOIRS

HILARIOUS M.B.A MEMOIRS

by

HARI HARA SUBRAMANIAN

PAPER TOWNS
PUBLISHERS

PAPER TOWNS
PUBLISHERS

First Published by
Paper Towns Publishers
72, Vishwanath Dham Colony,
Niwaru Road, Jhotwara,
Jaipur, 302012

HILARIOUS MBA MEMOIRS

ISBN Print Book - 978-93-6185-238-1

Printed in India

Acknowledgments

This book is dedicated to the three most important and beautiful women in my life- my mother, wife and daughter. To my dad – for his ability to live life as a happy-go-lucky soul and smile through turbulence. To all my friends and family without whom I wouldn't have had so many lovely memories which could form the basis for this memoir (Some names have been deliberately changed). To my school (St. John's Church), junior college (Narayana) and engineering college (Vasavi College of Engineering), for building resilience in me from an early age. To all the corporate organizations where I worked and the people I have interacted with, which helped me build my professional career. To Prince Augustine and Tanmoy Roy, for mentoring me during tricky situations in my corporate career. To the E. A role in particular, as this was the role where I used to draft zillions of emails for my most admired bosses – Veejay Nakra and Jyoti Malhotra, which helped develop my writing skills. To my mental health coaches – Dr. Venkatesh Babu, Dr. Anubhuti Upadhyay, and Dr. Akanksha Pandey – for helping me re-discover my passion. To Manik, Shivang and the entire publishing team of Paper Towns India for bringing this book to life. To my dear friend Vinay Poojary for designing a kick-ass cover for the book. To my amazing set of close friends (you know who you are) for everything you are and for being with me through thick and thin.

Last, but not least, to my alma mater, XLRI, which made me who am I today.

Contents

1

Rote Ministry (Ratt Sako toh Ratt Lo)

"Children – Please fill in the blanks - A for… … ?"

For the first 6 years of my life, I thought the only answer to this question was Apple, until one of my neighbors who was studying in Hyderabad Public School told me that A stands for Antelope. I couldn't stop laughing at his poor English. I proudly told him that I am from St. John's Church High School, and A stands for Apple, and always got full marks for writing this answer. Antelope was wrong, and his teacher doesn't know. After a few years, I figured out that a word called Antelope existed and I had made a royal fool out of myself all these years. None of us in our Kindergarten had bothered to question that there were multiple answers to "A for _______". Nor did our teachers bother to explain. We had just learnt, by rote, the letters of the alphabet proudly.

Ratta-Raj[1] continued not only for the first 6 years, but also the next 15 years. The first Hindi poem I had learnt by rote was "Hawa Chali[2]". It went something like this, "Hawa Chali, Kali Khili, Badal Garja, Paani Barsa, Bijli Chamki, Tanman Harsha, Raju Aaya, Chatha Laaya…. , Exam Ho gaya, Sab Kuch Bhool

[1] Rote Kingdom

[2] The Wind Blew

Gaya[3]." I had no idea what the words "Kali Khili" meant when I had written the poem in the exam. We were asked to write this poem in my kindergarten, and without understanding what the poem meant, I had mugged up every word, vomited it out and topped the Hindi paper. Not too many questions regarding doubts/clarifications were entertained in the classroom. The poor kids who used to ask questions would be scoffed at in the parent-teachers meeting - "The kid is not able to grasp, look at the number of questions he asks... *Ladka tej nahi hai isi liye sawaal karta hai*[4]. She needs to concentrate. Only then she will ask fewer doubts." Looking at this fate, most of us stopped asking questions during classes. We would blindly learn by rote, anything and everything, reproduce it like a Xerox copy, and score full marks. Looking at my report card and getting full marks for brilliantly reproducing "Hawa Chali" as it is to the last full stop without bothering to understand the complete meaning, I felt I had conquered Mount Everest. I also vividly remember *ratta-fying*[5] the concept of rain. I remembered the keywords EVAPORATION and CONDENSATION. I reproduced the lines in the text book and topped my science exam. Recently, my four-year-old niece asked me "how does rainfall happen?" Proud of my science topping achievements in school, I rattled off – "Rainfall has 2 steps – 1) Evaporation and 2) Condensation. In evaporation, the water in the ground dries up or evaporates in the air. This process continues until the drops of water become heavier and heavier. They become heavy and wind comes in the picture and shapes these drops of water into clouds."

---

[3] *Loosely translating to: The wind blew, the plants bloomed (kali khili), the clouds burst, rain drops came down, thunder struck, umbrellas came out, along with Raju... the exam was done, and the poem was forgotten*

[4] He's just not quick enough to grasp things.

[5] Learning by-rote

She asked me how can wind shape the drops of water. I proudly replied "Wind can take any direction. It wraps the air-filled water round and round, thus forming oval shaped clouds. Then, condensation happens. When the clouds become heavy, they are unable to withstand their weight. It is like filling a balloon with water. If you fill too much water, the balloon blasts. Similarly, after too much evaporated water is accumulated in the clouds, the clouds burst to form rain." My wife came running from behind hearing the last few lines and shoved me away. She pulled me into the bedroom and asked me to show my MBA degree certificate from XLRI Jamshedpur, one of India's best B schools. Suddenly, I could see Durga Maa[6] coming to life. Instantly, I reached into my "important documents" folder and showed her my XLRI degree certificate. Flabbergasted, she yelled at me – "Dude, how the hell did they allow you into XLRI when you don't know the process of rainfall." I calmly replied "Chill, Baby. They just didn't ask me this question in the interview. "

Not only Hindi and Science, even the English language was not spared in my school. In Andhra Pradesh, we had a subject called "*Special English*". Taking up that subject was supposedly meant to improve your English skills. And how? By ratta-fying the non-detail/supplementary text book. For example, in class 7, the additional text book of class 8 would be given to us to make our English "special". And 50% weightage in the exam was given to "Arrange the following sentences in chronological order. " Generally, the text book would be a novel –The Hound of Baskervilles, The Trojan War, The Adventures of Huckleberry Finn, etc. All fantastic books. But our job was

[6] Goddess Durga

to ensure we *ratta-fied*[7] the full book. Sentences from different chapters would be given and we were supposed to arrange them in the right sequence. For example - "Rank the following statements 1 to 10 in chronological order - 1. Stapleton killed Jonathan. 2 Jonathan was responsible for killing Maria. 3. Maria got poisoned. 4. Stapleton's wife went to the super market to buy poison…." How on earth are you supposed to remember all the chapters of a book in sequence? And passing the subject rested on your ability to RATTA. Ratt sako toh ratt lo…. [8]

The whole concept of reading a book, creating inferences by analyzing the characters, using the right grammar, was *not* there at all. The only thing Special about the Special English subject was we understood the meaning of the word "chronology". Again, the Britishers have a strange way of complicating things. Why can't we just use the word "sequence" and not have complicated synonyms for it, like chronology. And to everything there is a "logy" attached to it. Biology, Psephology,Analogy, Rama-logy, Sita-logy, Mentaal-ogy, Ghanta-logy!! Ridiculous. Therefore, we used to show off the word "chronology" to our neighbors. The worst part about the character analysis component in Special English was that we were given fixed answer notes by our teachers to go through, after each class. Any deviation from these notes in the exam answer sheet would mean we would not get full marks. I guess God had whispered in our state board schooling committee head's ears- "The only way for India to be a shining star in the New World Order is to ensure all your students speak English in the same way and are at an equal level of intelligence. Inspire them on these lines and they will become special at English." Therefore, the entire state board schooling

[7] Learnt by-rote

[8] Learn by-rote if you can

system in Hyderabad worked on the simple philosophy – "Joh Ratta marta hai, Woh Sikander Hai, Joh Sochta hai/Sawaal Poochtha Hai, woh Bandar Hai[9]."

Ratt-nama[10] didn't stop at school. It continued into the South Indian Sweatshop Business[11]. I enrolled myself into Ramayana Junior College – the answer to all my dreams. In those days, we had 2 outstanding junior colleges – Ramayana and Sri Anjaneya who used to publish front page ads of IIT[12] entrance exam toppers with captions on the lines of "Join Ramayana, Sure Shot Success Guaranteed.... Join Sri Anjaneya, it's no different than Ramayana." I chose to join Ramayana as the name reminded me of Lord Rama.

I thought I had entered the Kingdom of Dreams. Alas! That, in hindsight, was a distorted dream, I guess. Those were the most difficult 2 years of my existence in this Universe. I used to not do anything other than studying. No movies. No hanging out with friends. Monday to Friday would be classes and Saturday would be the exam and Monday would be another exam. I used to study for the exam in the bus, cram loads and loads of information in an overloaded tiny brain. I am sure Tihar jail must be having greater freedom inside, than these junior colleges. This wasn't even bonded labour. It felt like we paid, to get laid!

In 2002, the junior college fees were a staggering 40,000 INR for 2 years. The college timings – 8:00 am to 6:30 pm. After 6:30 was a counselling session. I thought counselling meant

---

[9] The rote-learner takes all

[10] Rote-ministry

[11] Hyperbole for the hard work which students put in class 11 and 12.

[12] The Indian Institutes of Technology – the numero uno school for pursuing under-grad in engineering and technology streams

speaking to the students, understanding their problems in life at that moment, etc. But no! Counselling in these sweat shops meant asking doubts for the concepts/syllabus/problems covered during the day. Heights of ridiculousness. I used to start at 7 am, and come home by 9 pm. Monday to Friday. And tests on Saturday and Monday.

The worst humiliation was – there was a periodic assessment and low performing students would be relegated to the next section where the experienced teachers would not go. I guess they took inspiration from the English Premier League- the only difference being English football relegates a club at the end of every year. These junior colleges *relegated* students every quarter. Truly Terrible Tales.

And again, the basic foundation was "RATTA". We ratta-fied formulas to ensure we answered multiple questions quickly. Speed thrills. . . and builds your skills! So, I ratta-fied Bernoulli's theorem, Laws of Thermodynamics, Charged Particles. The worst irony - Mathematics also started coming under Ratta. Physics, Chemistry was understandable. The maths teacher used to shout "(a+b-c)/ (f+g+h) to the power 43… pehchaan kaun [13]?" The students used to shout in chorus "0". The student who used to raise his hand first would be given a prize. Oh Jesus! So, I ratta-fied my way into engineering college. The sad part was about to follow. Amidst all this, I forgot to register for my IIT exam and I must be one of the few engineers in the history of India since Independence, who has not given an IIT entrance exam. I was busy preparing for the weekly Ramayana tests and forgot to register. Dhritharashtra ji of Jaane Bhi Do Yaaron (a 1983 Bollywood cult classic)

---

[13] Answer this question

must have been zapped and asked Duryodhan – "Beta, ye kyaa ho raha hai?[14]"

The final hammer blow which exposed my RATTA skills came recently. My wife was sitting on a bean bag.

She: "Honey, let's empty the bean bag."

Me: "But what happens if the beans fall out? Won't the beans smell rotten? And won't insects come?"

She: "What the hell are you blabbering?"

Me, with innocence: "I always thought that the bean bag was made of beans – the vegetable beans"

My wife looked towards the sky and pleaded "Hey Bhagwaan! Mujhe is RATTINDER SINGH sey peecha chudwa do please![15]"

---

[14] Son! What's going on?

[15] Oh God!! Please save me from this Rote Champion!

2

My First Crush (Mere Khayalon ki Mallika)

While St. John's Church High School was no way close to being the best school in Hyderabad, it had its own charm. The ratio of boys vs girls here was a mind-blowing 47: 5 (47 boys for every 5 girls). There could only be two hypotheses to this shocking stat. Hypothesis 1: Boys were the victims of our previous generation's probable dislike for raising girl child. Hypothesis 2: Girl parents used to be scared about their children joining our rowdy school. In those days, the Secunderabad -Marredpally area had 5 schools. Keyes and St. Ann's were "girls-only" schools (which seemed to eliminate hypothesis 1), while St. Patrick's and St. Mary's were "boys- only" school. Ours was the only co-ed school on paper.

Despite these challenges, the brave hearts of St. John's never complained. So, what if the ratio was 47: 5? The boys in our school believed "united we stand, but the last man standing takes it all", even if it comes to having a crush.

We can never forget our first crush, can we? There was a beautiful girl by the beautiful name Mallika. The whole school had a crush on her. True to her name, Mallika was literally an angel. She had curly hair, a sweet smile, was reasonably tall, and svelte (in case Fair & Lovely had come here for an audition, she would have won it hands down). She was an all-rounder; she was the sports captain and good in academics (Imagine this; we were 3 years junior to her but we used to get updates about her rank in class every month).

Friday evenings, she used to practice throwball and the whole school would converge to see her in action as though Deepika Padukone was playing throwball. Once she left, the place would be immediately vacated (like how crowds in the 90s would vacate the stadium immediately after Sachin got out). When she used to practice cricket near the canteen, the whole school would be standing at mid-wicket, waiting for a catch. Boys used to push each other and dive in vain to impress Mallika with their fielding prowess.

Kuch log alag level key dorey daaltey they. [16] They would offer her gloves and show her the various wrist positions of batting. The other boys would be teething with anger and jealousy looking at these *dorey-baaz*[17]. In those days, even though she played practice matches with under-arm bowling, there was a tacit understanding amongst all the boys in the school – the bowlers, fielders and spectators that they would not allow her to get out. If some other girl came to bat, they would immediately bowl a fast under-arm ball and either get that girl bowled or caught. But when Mallika was batting, the boys would bowl at their slowest, catch only on one bounce. It was a win-win situation for all the stakeholders. Mallika would get more and more match practice, the rest would just have fun watching the beautiful Mallika practice.

---

[16] Some people would go the extra mile to flirt with her.

[17] Flirts

In those days, we would look forward to exam halls. In exam halls, we would always sit next to our seniors, to prevent copying. Everyone would secretly hope that they would get to sit next to Mallika. A few lucky ones would brag about this achievement, watching Mallika write her exams for 3 hours. I, though, had no such luck. I always used to envy those chaps. I had heard of certain schools having double promotion for academically brilliant students. I secretly hoped that I would get a triple promotion so that we both were in the same class.

A few despos from our class went a mile ahead. Even though she was 3 years senior, after each exam was done, when Mallika would walk out of the exam hall, these folks would have the audacity and ask "Mallika, kaisa gaya exam?[18]" This would infuriate me even further. I used to frown and think "Arey mere tharki raja, mujhe kabhi poocha nahi exam kaisa gaya. Maine tum logon ko concepts padhaya hain. Aur Mallika key exam mey bada interest hai bey tum ko.... Kaisa ghor kalyug hai![19]"

I always waited for an opportunity to talk to her. *Talking* to her would be a big achievement in itself, as I could boast about it to my friends. Guys who could talk to her, including the jokers who asked "exam kaisa gaya Mallika", were considered as the cool dudes of our school. I always secretly wanted to talk to her and be a cool dude, but never did anything worthy of being one. The closest I came to become a cool dude was when I deliberately ran fast while Mallika was walking in front of me. I stopped, turned behind and looked over Mallika's shoulder and shouted "Abey Pramod, tum mujhe nahi pakad paaye[20]. I am

---

[18] How did your exam go?"

[19] My Despo Friend- I have taught you so many concepts before exams, but you never bothered to ask me how my exam went. But a sudden interest in Mallika's exam

[20] Hey Pramod, you couldn't catch me.

too fast for you guys." Mallika conveniently ignored, I guess she had seen too many jokers playing such cheap tricks.

When I was in class 6, we had shifted to a house close to our school. Lady Luck finally seemed to have smiled on me. While playing cricket, I hit a ball in the opposite house. I went inside searching for the ball. Suddenly, the door opened. A sweet-sounding voice asked "What do you need?" I didn't reply. Then, the curtain opened. I could not believe my eyes. It was Mallika. I wanted to extend the conversation but didn't know how to. Sheepishly, I answered - "My name is Hari and I am from 6 A. I study in St. John's School. I think I have seen you play cricket. We have just shifted here. Is there a power cut in your house as well? My mom asked me to find out. " I had no idea why I said these words. Mallika smiled and said "No, not at our place, but yes, this area is prone to power cuts. Is there anything else I can help you with?" I replied- "No. But thanks a lot, as we have just shifted, will keep taking your help if required." She smiled and said "Sure. Always happy to help."

I was thrilled. I forgot about the cricket ball and came back. My friends asked me about the ball. I told them I could not find the ball. I cared a damn about the ball, I had struck a sixer in my "cool dude innings". I was delighted. The next few moments, I was lost in the below thoughts.

Scenario 1: Me and Mallika would have started talking more often. I would daily bluff and take Maths tuition or Hindi tuition from her. In the pretext of a tuition, I would get to admire her from close quarters for a longer time.

Scenario 2: Me and Mallika would be walking towards home after school and we would be chatting about movies, music and our lives.

Scenario 3: I would learn cycling from Mallika. She would patiently see me learn cycling and in case I was about to fall, she would come and hold me.

Scenario 4: On my birthday, Mallika would give me a cricket bat saying – "This is for a special person" and as a return gift, I would gift her a teddy bear and she would pinch me on the cheeks – "How cute of you, Hari!!"

Scenario 5: I imagined myself to be Chandrachur Singh, and Mallika was Aishwarya Rai from the Bollywood movie Josh. I would give a rose to her and sing – "Mere Khayaalon ki mallika… chaaro taraf teri chaiyya rey…thaam le aake baiyaa."

I was staring at her house and was about to think of a few more scenarios, when someone patted me from behind and said loudly "Arey Hari, tu idhar shift ho gaya. . . Aai Shaabaash!![21]" This Aai Shaabaash was a familiar voice. I turned around and was pleasantly surprised to see Arjun, my good friend from school (who was a year junior to me). Arjun and me were very good friends and we used to play cricket in school. I wanted to tell him that I had made my first move in becoming a cool dude and had spoken to Mallika for a couple of minutes. I wanted to tell him about my plan of the birthday gift, the return gift, the Math tuition strategy, and ask for a few ideas from his as well. I was about to start explaining all these thoughts but he interrupted "Hari bhai, glad that you are now my neighbor. I stay right opposite your house, along with my elder sister, Mallika. We also have two elder brothers, who are well built pahalwaans[22]."

I could not believe these words. I was hoping this was not true. How could I not know this? Arjun was Mallika's younger

---

[21] Hey Hari. You shifted here? Congrats

[22] Muscular men, resembling bouncers in a pub

brother. Thank God he was not in my class, or else it would have been very embarrassing to reveal about your crush to her younger brother. In that very moment, my dreams of becoming friends with my crush got crushed. To add insult to injury, I was also told about the pehelwaani bodyguards. Mallika was in Class X that year and we could not see much of her in either throwball or cricket practice. We all mourned in silence that year when it was announced that the students of class X had finished their exams and had become alumni.

Mallika's departure had left a million hearts wounded. I never saw or heard of Mallika after that. Arjun had shifted his house that very year, so he ceased to be our neighbor. Neither did we have Facebook or WhatsApp in those days. Slowly and steadily, in a few months' time, Mallika vanished from our heart, mind and soul. That year, we felt a sense of emptiness. We did not know what to do. The cricket and throwball practice became a dull affair, so did the exams. We all wanted Mallika back. We all prayed to God, hoping a miracle would happen. But God did not allow it. God had other plans in store for us, though.

The following year, while in class 9, another beautiful girl joined us. She had come from another school. She was an extrovert and spoke to everyone. She would introduce herself with a handshake and say – "Hi, I am Raagini!!" That was it. The more things try to change, the more they remain the same. Mallika was forgotten in an instant. The circus started again. Cricket practice, throwball practice, attempts to take tuition. "Raagini, exam kaisa gaya? Ghar mey powercut hai[23]", "Can I do combined study in your house?", "Can I borrow your notes?", "Can I play badminton with you?", etc.

I guess boys will be boys, and men will be men. Always!

---

[23] How did your exam go? There's a power cut in my house

3

Genuine Jockey

After our tryst with the likes of Mallika and Raagini in school, we entered junior college with high hopes of finding our life partners. We had always grown up to movies where the hero meets his life partner in college and has an amazing life with bike rides, movie shows, and parties. Unlike St. John's Church High School, in those days, Ramayana Junior College was one of the best colleges with an excellent gender ratio (we were told that girls outnumbered boys). On the basis of some extensive market research, all of us had figured out that the main head office branch in Vittalwadi area had the most beautiful girls enrolling. Vittalwadi was about 15 kms from my house in Marredpally, but I convinced my parents that it was the best branch and I would take a 45-minute bus journey with a change-over so that I could gain *access* to the best education!

The first 15 minutes of my first day at Ramayana Junior College was quite an experience. I had reached the main building and was pleasantly surprised to see myself surrounded by an army of girls. I first thought I had come to a "girls-only" college, so I went and checked with the watchman on the same. He seemed to have read my mind and smiled mischievously, "Saab[24], I have good news and bad news for you. The good news

[24] Sir

is that this *is* Ramayana Junior College." He paused for a minute. I thought that finally God had smiled and all the strategies I had formulated to woo Mallika could be executed here. I was about to get lost in these dreams when the watchman interrupted me again "Saab, the bad news is... this is the Main Building, which is a "girls-only" building. For the boys, there is another building 2 kms away; it is called "Sick" Building." I was crest-fallen. My bad luck continued.

I consoled myself and walked the long walk from Main Building to the "Sick" Building. What a sick experience it was. The walk was excruciatingly long and painful. I reached the gate of the building. I met a tall guy (he looked like a senior). I asked him curiously, "Excuse me!! Is this Sick Building? If yes, why is this called Sick Building? Was there a hospital here before, which used to treat sick patients?" He burst out laughing "Bro, what's your name? You seem to be a funny chap. It is not "Sick" building, bro. It is "Sikh" building. The building is owned by a Sikh and the building is besides a gurudwara. By the way, my name is Khaled Zaki. I am in class 12. Welcome to Sikh building." I thanked Khaled and moved on.

Those two years at Sikh Building were the most *harassing* two years of my life. We used to cram loads and loads of information with the only aim to get great ranks in the state board and IIT entrance exams. We felt we were being roasted in a sauce-pan, like chickens. The only thing we used to look at, for 10 hours in a day, was the blackboard. Formulas after formulas, short cut methods, cheap answer-memorizing tricks for remembering chemical reactions... the list was endless. 75% of the time was spent with senior lecturers, the balance 25% by a rare specimen called *Junior lecturers*. These folks would not allow us to go out of the class and have water at the watercooler. They were scared that we would use this to walk out of the class and enjoy the outside world. Saturdays and Sundays (days of the weekly Multiple-Choice Question (MCQ) tests), which are supposed to be happy weekends, would be like Sales month-end closings. We wished they never existed, but there was no other alternative than to live through the hell, hoping "this too shall pass." I am told that investment banking jobs and consulting jobs have the least work-life balance, apart from Sales & Customer Care related jobs. People who crib about work-life balance issues in the corporate world should spend a month shadowing a student of the junior colleges in the South. They will go back and never utter a word about work-life balance. There was neither work, nor life! It was only preparation. Prepare, prepare and prepare. The fear of being relegated to a junior class made it intensely competitive. It was literally a dog-eat-dog world, the only exception being there were plenty of dogs (me included) with no time to eat.

Every action has an equally opposite reaction. Amidst all this artificially induced stressful ecosystem, the Sikh building class of 2004, after the first year (class 11) decided to take matters into their own hands and find ways to de-stress. If a class was getting too serious, somebody would deliberately drop a tiffin box on the floor while the professors were busy scribbling on the blackboard. When the professor would turn towards us, everyone would shout in chorus "Aawwwwww." The professor would yell in anger "If it happens again, I will throw that scoundrel out!" As soon as he would turn towards the board, another tiffin box would be deliberately dropped. This time, the whole class would clap in unison. This professor was a gem at heart, though. He would never complain to the higher authorities. I guess he understood that we were using his class as a proxy to relieve us from the stress.

Amidst all this, we came to know that Khaled Zaki was featured amongst the top 10 rank-holders in the state. It was a proud moment for all of us as his photo was published in the front page. Sikh Building suddenly came into limelight as one of the Ramayana branches which could produce heroes. What this also meant was that the expectations from the current batch were also high. This resulted in more practice papers, more cramming, more hard work for all of us. My favorite memory of Ramayana Junior College, though, was just about to come. Our physics professor, Rajesh Kumar was quite a character. RK, as he was called, had a very weird way of pronunciation. A parachute would be called out loudly by him as "pyara-ch**th", topper as "taaappar", apple as "yaapil", auto as "aato". Poor RK would not realize that he was becoming a joke with his pronunciations. However, RK was a very strict prof, which made it very difficult for students to laugh in his class. All of us would use laughter-camouflaging tactics to escape his wrath. Some would bite their tongue, some would put a pen in between their teeth and bite, some would just throw a book below the desk, bend down and laugh.

During one of RK's physics class, I was sitting beside my best friend, Arun Vijaya Kumar (he introduced himself as AVK à la SRK). RK started off, "Dear students, we are proud to inform you that we have our very own student from Sikh Building who has stood Rank 7 in the state entrance exams. He's your senior. Any guesses what's his name?"

Students knew the answer, but they didn't want to tell it out loud. That was their way of showing respect to RK. RK continued "Friends – the gentleman is none other than a person named... Khaled Jockey!!" That was it! RK had pronounced Zaki as "Jockey". Beside me was the burly, 80+ kgs AVK. We couldn't control our laughter. AVK kept his hand on the desk, bent downwards so that he could see the floor, and started thumping the desk continuously, like the way politicians thump their desk in parliament. The whole desk was vibrating, as if hit by an earthquake. Looking at AVK's laughter, a few others burst out laughing. I just looked at RK, and laughed in his face, thanks to the Jockey word and AVK's even more hilarious reaction. RK, meanwhile, was fuming. He came up to us and asked us to stand on the bench. That was his standard way of humiliating people. AVK was least bothered about all of this. He continued to stand up on the bench and continued to shriek hysterically in laughter. RK, who was of a short build, was now seething in anger. He tried to beat AVK on his shoulder. AVK continued to laugh. Before RK could lay his hands on AVK's shoulder, AVK (who, at 6 feet and 80 kgs, was way too strong for RK's 5 feet and 45 kgs) caught him by his hand and pushed RK back. The class could not control their laughter. It was the best de-stressor they could have asked for.

The consequences of this incident were huge. Me and AVK were not allowed to attend the Physics class indefinitely till we brought our parents and have them apologize to RK on behalf of us. We were too scared and embarrassed to get our parents into the picture. So, daily, for the next 30 days, me and AVK used to walk out of RK's class and stand outside for the whole duration of the class. Finally, RK relented and accepted our apology. Since then, me and AVK decided that we will never sit next to each other.

Till this date, whenever I pass by a Jockey store, I can't help remember Khaled Zaki, RK and AVK. In those days, "Genuine Jockey" was the tagline for the Jockey brand of undergarments. RK, AVK and Khaled Zaki were jockeyed genuinely in my memories.

4

The Ides of March

While Khaled "Jockey" made us proud by securing Rank 7 in the state entrance exams, I was nowhere close to it. My rank of 1078 made me get admission into Vasavi Engineering College.

Life was one hell of a roller-coaster ride. I learnt to eat a burger the right way (The first time I was exposed to a burger, I had eaten it like an idli[25], tearing off parts of it one by one, only to see my friends dying of laughter in the bakery). When I was small, one of the astrologers in Tirupati had predicted that I would be having two marriages. Therefore, I decided that I would avoid getting into a relationship commitment at such an early stage in life. However, I used to observe the famous "campus couples".

In most cases, the boyfriend in the relationship would be more of a personal assistant to the girl. *Notes likhwana, canteen sey khana lana, driver ban-ke sightseeing karwana, mobile recharge, heels dilwana*[26]. These used to be some of the key roles and responsibilities. It was such an expensive exercise, I felt. Some matches, though, were made in heaven and we felt that the

---

[25] Idli is a soft & fluffy steamed cake made of fermented rice & lentil batter

[26] Writing class notes, getting food from the canteen, being a driver and helping in sightseeing, buying heels

boyfriends who made all these errands were finally rewarded with love for life.

However, the ides of March would strike every year. I could never forget my March memories. Around the 15th of March 2006, I got out *hit wicket* in the loo. It was the penultimate class of Electronic Theory. Our professor had made a seemingly simple topic very complicated with fuzzy equations. None of us could understand a word. The professor didn't care, though, and went on and on and completed the course, without bothering to check if the students had understood the concept. After the class got over, Sandeep (one of my close friends) and I started to bitch about the Prof in the loo. Sandeep started off "Uski maa ki aankh. . Kaisa gadha hai. . Samajh icch nahi aata bava. . Bole jaa raha tha Bole jaa raha tha. . Item no. 1 Prof hai bava![27]" I nodded, "Aisey professors ko suli pey latkana chahiye. Hagne mey ustaad hai saaley[28] ..." As soon as I uttered these words, the door of one of the closed toilets opened, and The Professor came out and smiled mischievously. Me and Sandeep smiled for a second and ran away. I thought to myself *"Mooh band nahi rakhoge jab kar rahe ho moothi, to tumhari life ban jayegi ek bahut badi tatti[29]."*

A year later, in March 2007, we were having our "industry" visit in Goa. Our forefathers (read seniors) in Vasavi had figured out a company called D-link in Goa, and every batch used to visit Goa. The best part was only 2 people in a batch of 60 would visit this factory and the rest would note down the same learnings. All hell broke loose that day in my first "banana ride". The banana ride was in groups of five, and me being an

---

[27] What an Idiot. He kept on ranting but none of us could understand

[28] Such Profs should be sentenced. They are experts at sh*tting

[29] If you can't keep your mouth shut while peeing, then your life will become a big piece of sh*t

"enthu-cutlet" since childhood, I volunteered amongst the first batch. It felt thrilling to sit on a tube and go into the middle of the sea. Like a Bollywood Hero, I started waving back to my friends, with one hand held on the tube. I did not realize what was coming next. The tube boat overturned and here I was, going down into the ocean. I thought I was going into the depths of the ocean. I could see only bubbles of the ocean bed as I was vertically going downwards. I closed my eyes and thought I was gone. Three seconds later, my friend, Harshad, was shouting "You idiot! You are wearing a life-jacket, so nothing will happen. Just float and go back to the tube!"

Instead of going back to the tube, I went to Harshad and caught hold of him like a breastfeeding baby, which holds tightly to its mother. I had turned pale white, and Harshad was frantically annoyed. The boat instructor had already spent 30 minutes trying to instruct me to let go of Harshad's hand and go back to the tube. Both of us were floating in the middle of the sea, and now it was turning dark. Harshad, being the character that he was, finally started laughing "Abey *gadhe ki aulaat*[30], you don't drown if you have the life-jacket on you. We have two options. Like jokers, we keep hugging each for the entire day, or we go back." Until then, I had never seen a lifejacket nor understood its properties. Harshad's words brought some sense in me, relieved me of my panic, and we returned. I thought I would be given a hero's welcome for trying out a daring experiment. Instead, I was welcomed with loud guffaws all around.

The biggest blow, though, was saved for March 2008. We were in our final year. I was bored of reading up before every exam for four consecutive years and decided to do some dare-

[30] Son of a Donkey

devilry. Inspired by my friend Dilip, I decided to use "chits" to pass off the exam. It was the easiest short-cut. "Digital Signal Processing" was a pretty drab subject and I was least interested in knowing the various theories and flow diagrams. Each flow diagram would carry 20 marks. Dilip was the "chit-master" and he used to effortlessly use the chits and get the same marks as me. He used to never get caught, though. The girls were impressed by his finesse. I decided to take matters in my own hands. I was scared to open a chit in front of the invigilator and copy brazenly. So, I decided to use a "disruptive innovation". I used my hand-kerchief as my "Brahmastra[31]".

Every now and then, I would fake a sneeze and use my handkerchief to wipe my nose. I would then keep the handkerchief under my desk and in the pretext of wrapping it, I would look at the chit and draw my flow charts. I could have sneezed twice, copied two flow charts and submitted the paper. It would have helped me pass the exam. But my male libido got the better off me and I wanted to impress the girls and boast of full marks when I walked out. I wanted to be one up over Dilip. So, I sneezed every 10 minutes and continued the sneeze-open handkerchief – copy – fold handkerchief routine. By the time, I sneezed for the sixth time, the invigilator came to and asked concerningly – "Beta, allergy ho gayi kya aapko[32]... Why don't you step out and come back?" I panicked. In my panic, the handkerchief fell off the desk and a whole bunch of chits fell on the invigilator's shoes. The invigilator was seething in anger "You scoundrel!! I really thought you had a bad cold!! I am going to tear up your answer sheet and hand you over to the H. O. D!"

---

[31] In ancient Sanskrit writings, Brahmashtra was an Astra (weapon) created by Lord Brahma

[32] Son,looks like you have an allergy

I immediately remembered Salman and Aamir from Andaz Apna Apna[33] I wanted to say – "Sir, hum to bachche hain, mann key sacche, nakal key kacche.. aap purush hi nahi ... mahapurush ho ... mahapurush[34]." I was about to fall at his feet and pull out his shoes. The invigilator told me "I could have cancelled your hall ticket but because you have begged me, I will just give you a zero." That was my first and last zero in my academic career. Dilip had warned me a few days ago that I may get into trouble copying as I had not done it before, but I had not paid to his warning. The Ides of March had stuck ... again.

The month of March continued to haunt me. I had cleared my XAT[35] written test a year later and had got calls from XLRI for both the Business Management (BM) course and the Human Resources Management (HRM) course. My first choice was BM, as in those days, I used to foolishly think that HR was only for ladies as most of the HR folks were women. On March 15th 2009, I walked confidently into my XLRI BM interview. Three Professors stared at me as I took my chair. I hated my electronics course and I prayed to God that I would not be asked any questions on academics. I had prepared well on questions like why MBA, why Business Management, latest Current Affairs topics, short-term goals and long-term goals. I had managed 78% in my engineering but I had lost interest in electronics engineering mid-way. The Big Apple[36] didn't interest me, so I ruled out the GRE exam unlike most folks from Andhra and therefore, I wanted to do my MBA.

The interview started.

---

33 Hit Bollywood comedy

34 Sir...we are naïve young kids. You are like God to us.

35 Admissions test for the MBA program of XLRI Business School.

36 The USA

Professor 1: "Hari, you seem to have got a fantastic academic record. I am assuming you are thorough in your academic concepts ..."

Me, confidently: "Yes, Sir"

I didn't realize that I had made a mistake by lying. Immediately, Professor 2 got interested and started off "Great. Even I am an electronics graduate. Tell me, what is the difference between normal diode and Zener diode?"

Me "Sir, Zener diode has some special properties which are opposite to a normal diode. "

Professor 2: "Go on"

Me: "That's it, Sir. I can't remember more, Sir"

Professor 2: "Never mind. Can you tell me the difference between P-N-P transistor and N-P-N transistor?"

Me: "Sir. . . PNP and NPN are opposites. Likes attract. Opposites repel. + multiplied by + = + Negative multiplied by negative is also positive. So, all transistors are positive sir"

Professor 3: "Excellent, and thank you, Sir. You may leave. We are done!" That was my shortest interview ever. Less than 3 minutes. For a 3-minute interview, I had taken a flight from Hyderabad to Chennai, stayed in a hotel for a day, read the morning newspaper, prepared a lot for "Why MBA?", but all this was of no use. Again, I had ignored my senior Vineeth's advice of going through my academic courses. I hated the electronics course, but I didn't know that I would continue to be haunted.

I felt like Virender Sehwag[37], in his debut one day match. He walked in, got an in-swinging Yorker from Shoaib Akhtar, got wrapped in his pads and walked back without even looking at the umpire to signal LBW. Sehwag had spent more time walking to the crease and back rather than at the crease. However, Sehwag had got another chance and he became the legendary Sehwag. I hoped my HR interview would not go the same way.

To this day, the Ides of March haunt me. I never schedule anything important around the 15th of March.

[37] Former India cricketer

5

Diamonds are Forever (Heera Hai Sada Key Liye)

Thankfully, my XLRI HR interview was a good 10 days after the 15th of March and I was not asked any academic questions, unlike my BM fiasco. The interview was a relaxed one. Excerpts from the interview:

Prof: “Do you know today’s breaking news?”

Me: “Yes, Sir. The Sri Lankan cricket team narrowly escaped a bomb blast in Pakistan, and they are returning”

Prof: “Excellent Any other word you know which can be used for “breaking news”?”

Me: “Dhamaaka, sir”

Prof: “Any other alternative?”

Me: “*Sansani-khej khulaasa* sir”

Prof: “What’s your favorite news channel?”

Me: “Aaj Tak, sir… sorry, sir. NDTV. ”

Prof: “You seem to be confused?”

Me: “No, sir. In English, its NDTV, In Hindi, it’s Aaj Tak ”

Both of us sheepishly smiled at each other after my answer.

Prof: "Are you aware of the term human capital?"

Me, confidently: "Yes, sir. I am not aware, sir"

Prof: "It's ok. At least you are honest. Can you guess which countries must be having high human capital?"

Me: "India and China, maybe, sir."

Prof: "If you are a HR manager, and apart from India and China, you want to hire people from countries with high capital, which would be your next two countries?"

Me: "Pakistan and Bangladesh, sir"

Prof: "Thank you, sir"

This abrupt "Thank you sir" reminded me of my BM interview. But at least I was happy that the interview went on for about 15 to 20 minutes and I was not clean bowled first ball. When the results got out, I was waitlisted 24. Like an IRCTC[38] traveller (in those days, there was no e-tatkal[39] option), who prays to God that his ticket gets converted to RAC[40] so that he boards the train, I prayed to all the Gods in the world. Once my waitlist cleared, I did 108 *pradakshanams*[41] in the Chilkur Balaji temple, gave my hair at Tirupati and did *archanas*[42] in all my regular temples. I had finally become somebody in life and got entry into the *hallowed* portals of XLRI.

---

38 Indian Railways

39 Fast-track wait list clearance

40 Reservation after Cancellation

41 Rounds

42 Special prayers

Once I set foot into XLRI, life changed. I was told that getting into XLRI was not enough. It was *critical* to bag a good summer placement, build your CV by being part of committees, events etc. The same old story. In class 5, they said Class 7 was critical. After Class 7, class 10 became critical. Then class 12, then UG, then MBA. Once inside MBA, summer internship placements were critical. I got fed up of the word critical. The critical stuff didn't stop at summer placements. Once you got a summer placement, they said the summer project was critical. Then job. Then in job, first two years. I sometimes felt I should get admitted in the critical ICU ward of a hospital so that people just put an end to the critical syndrome.

Life was anything but a cakewalk in the first trimester at XL. My committee interviews were a disaster. I applied to every committee, got interviewed and got rejected. I never knew why though. The last committee left was the *Infracom* (library and mess management committee). Even the seniors in that committee also found others better than me. I thought to myself "Mess committee ka bhi layak nahi hoon. . Issey accha toh Hyderabad mey mess khol deta ... At least wahan toh izzat milta ...[43]"

The worst was yet to come. The summer internship placements were fast approaching. I was told that building a good CV is super *critical.* I initially did not understand what this whole CV building fuss was all about. My friends would spend minutes, hours and months *making* a *CV.* "Abey, khelne chalega... Nahi yaar CV bana raha hoon. . . Abey, canteen

[43] Not even worthy of being selected in the mess (hostel food management) committee. A better thing would be to open a mess of my own. I would be more respected in case of the latter.

chalega... Nahi yaar CV bana raha hoon[44]!" I did not pay much importance to this CV making business. I just made a plain jane CV in about 60 minutes and uploaded it. I never knew that this would cost me dearly.

The great Indian B school circus (read summer internship placements) started. 20 companies in day 0, 30 in day 1, 50 in day 2. 100 companies in 3 days. It was like a herd of sheep walking together. If one sheep would get poked, the whole herd would dance. If one person got interviewed, the rest of the herd would *gherao*[45] him "Abey kyaa poocha. . kya jawaab diya. . interviewer *maal* thi kya[46]?" I was like Buddha, unfazed by this circus as I got only 2 shortlists in the first 100 companies. One of those was Aditya Birla Group, a very reputed and respected company. I had been told in my practice mock GDs that I needed to speak more and be *aggressively participative* in my GDs. So, I got my chance and let loose like a raging bull in the GD and spoke for 5 out of 8 minutes in the GD. I was promptly eliminated. The next company was Reckitt Benckiser (RB). There was no GD. It was only an interview. I still don't know why RB and ABG shortlisted my CV and the remaining 98 did not. The RB interview was going well until it came to one question.

Interviewer: "Why HR?"

My seniors had warned me not to give childishly fake answers like "I love interrr-aaaacting with people". They had asked me to be genuine and confident.

---

[44] Will you come to play? Will you come to the canteen? No mate. ! I am making my CV

[45] Encircle

[46] What was asked? What did you answer? Was the interviewer a hot chick?

Me: "Sir, I had BM and HR calls. BM didn't clear, HR cleared. Hence HR. But now I am liking HR, sir"

Interviewer: "So HR was a compromise choice for you?"

Me: "No, Sir. It was my best convert, sir, and I didn't want to repeat a year giving MBA entrance exams"

The interviewer smiled. I returned the smile. Both of us knew that I had got *run out.* Not every interviewer likes an honest answer. Some like to listen to what they want to listen. I had got stumped in "Why HR?"

Later, I asked my friend who had cleared the interview. I asked him "Arey yaaar. , what did you answer for why HR?"

He said "Sach bataoon. . mujhe woh question kisine poocha hi nahi[47]." I cursed my bad luck.

With 3 days and 100 companies gone, 2 shortlists, a hit wicket out GD and "Why HR" run out interview, I decided to do some serious introspection. I started looking at CVs of my friends who got placed and exited the process. I was shocked to see the level of exaggeration of simple activities in the CV.

Someone who had won a carrom competition would glorify it as "Won a closely fought carrom competition from a pool of 60 participants, which were filtered from a town of population 2 crore (1. 2 crore male, 0. 8 crore female). Received a certificate from the Head Master of the college, which is the best college amongst the 20 lakh colleges in the country. "

Others who did not win anything but participated in something, would write "Made it to the final 64 list of

---

[47] To tell the truth, I was not asked that question at all.

participants from a pool of 23 crore morons and thus got appreciation from the senior- most faculty, who had no other pastime but to appreciate me for my glorious achievement. "

The best exaggerations would be the ones who organized college fests "Conceptualized, designed, strategized, executed, ideated and masturbated over the best-ever college fest in the world. Personally, went door to door like a Harpic salesman and ensured a superb turnout of 20,000 jokers as audience."

Some folks would do an environmental impact analysis of their achievements "Won the best student award* in graduation for all-round abilities. The best in all aspects from a batch of 6000. ("*" in small font meant I was the best farter). This led to a release of 3 micrograms of carbon-di-oxide in a fast-depleting ozone layer, thus generating a potential saving of 43, 659 kiloliters of green-house gas in the atmosphere."

Everyone in B school conceptualized college fests, everyone was the best all-rounder in college, everyone had the coolest hobbies, everyone was the sports captain, all except me. I had missed this CV glorification. Everything in life – farting, pooping, brushing, bathing, was converted into a glorified CV point with a percentile or relative grading. Now, I understood why my seniors were saying "It's important to *make* a good CV." I immediately got into action. I had scored centum in Maths Class 12. So, I changed it to "State Rank 1 from a pool of 35 lac test takers in Class 12 Mathematics." Instead of tech-fest organizer, I changed it to "Chief Creative Head – Tech Fest, responsible for conceptualizing, strategizing and designing the entire event end-to-end. Event was attended by 1000+ students from across India." I updated my CV on these lines and sent it to the Placement Committee. Immediately, a few seniors commented "Kya faadu CV hai bhai[48]." I was now back in business. I missed the first 100 companies but now in the next 30 companies, I was getting shortlisted everywhere. I still don't know if this was due to my CV innovation or because I was amongst only 20 folks left to get placed...

Then came the dreaded Group Discussion. As we were the last few folks left to be placed, each GD was like a dog-fight. Our GD environment resembled Jayanagar[49] 9th block at 5 am. We were like a bunch of sex-starved dogs ready to hump anyone (including the moderator) coming our way. Each of us would interject the other, rephrase the other's point, add, subtract, delete and make the GD as miserable as possible. It was literally torture. I tried various strategies – aggression, assertion, moderation, balance, initiative, conclusion, but none of it worked. I wanted to kill those people who invented this group discussion. The topics were crappy "Art is science made easy... All that glitters is not gold. . . Go to hell jokers and take your gold along. . . Screw you morons. . ."

There was one Group Discussion which I will never forget. The topic was "Gold vs Diamond". There was a Sardar who just wrote this topic on the board and smiled at all of us. We didn't know what to do first. The Sardar just smiled at all of us and said "That's the topic for discussion. . . Gold vs Diamond ... please start the discussion. You folks have already lost a minute. "

We were a total of 8 dogs in the GD. Dog 1 started "In ancient scriptures like Panchatantra, kings used to dig gold. Diamonds were never mentioned. So, gold is better. " Wild Dog

---

[48] What a terrific CV

[49] A locality in Bangalore, South India

2 rattled away "Gold is heavily traded and is used as an investing tool by crores of people. I agree with dog 1's point that Gold is better." Deranged Dog 3 interjected "Adding to both these points, I can recollect my grandmother handing over her gold necklace to me in childhood. Marriages in South have a huge display of gold. Hence Gold is better." I didn't know what to do. I blabbered "Folks, if you look at all the top actresses – Aishwarya, Katrina, Kareena – they all advertise for diamonds. Diamonds are forever and rare. Anything which is scarce, has higher value. In India, we don't value water compared to oil, as water is available. So, I think diamonds are better."

That was the only point I made in the GD. After that, people started leaning towards diamond. Before we could reach to a consensus, the sardar called off the GD.

15 minutes later, the results were announced. Me and one other guy, who also spoke only once in the GD, were the only two folks shortlisted for the interview round. I was puzzled.

The sardar smiled at me and said "Do you know why I shortlisted you? Because you spoke less but you spoke logically. I liked your logic"

I was thrilled. He continued "Why do you want to join my company?" I had just mugged up about the company a minute ago (my seniors had given me a one-pager). Until then, I hadn't heard of it. I bragged "Sir, working in a start-up like environment gives me the space to work on new ideas"

The Sardar was impressed "Great. I am done. You have any questions for me?" I replied "Sir, why HR?" The Sardar smiled and said "Young man, to be honest, I had two calls – BM and HR. I converted HR and so I joined. I liked HR so I continued in this profession. It's not for the weak-hearted. Congratulations. You have been selected."

I was relieved. I had gotten out of the chaotic placement process in the most random manner. I thought to myself - "*Heera hai sada key liye*[50]. *Cheers.*"

---

[50] Diamonds are forever

6

Amar, Akbar, Anthony, & Zuckerberg

Thanks to the "diamond" GD, I had got out of the summer internship process. Whenever I think of investing in SIPs (Systematic Investment Plans), I can't dread but think of the dreadful SIP (Summer Internship Process) at XL. It was quite a stressful process for most of us. My friend, *Bhai* (he resembles anyone but Bhai[51], he used to have thick spectacles and a proud paunch), was giving interviews with multiple companies every hour. He was not clearing the interviews though, despite quite a few shortlists.

I remember him sitting in a Pepsi interview. The poor guy was trying to get out of the placement process like every one of us. He had given an excellent interview and the interviewer asked him "Do you have any questions?" In his bid to impress the recruiter, he shot off to the *Pepsi* HR "Ma'am, how does a typical day look like at *Johnson & Johnson*?"

That was it. A single word pushed him from day 1 to day 2. Poor Bhai. *Tez banne gaye they*[52], but HR ultimately had the last laugh. Finally, he got through some HR consulting company on the last day after quite a torrid time. The placement process in

[51] Salman Khan

[52] Tried to act smart

B schools had taken its toll on *Bhai* as well. In fact, quite a few couples got "re-arranged" after the placement process. The guys who got through in day 0 companies, suddenly walked away with the beautiful girls. Quite a revelation.

Post our internship, life was a breeze. We thought so until we came into term 3. There we came face to face with the three Profs whose courses were considered to be the toughest- Amar, Akbar and Anthony. Amar used to teach Financial Management. *Inkey course mey maximum students amar ho jate they*[53]. Passing in this course was quite an achievement. 20 classes had 20 assignments. In each class, one set of assignments (students whose roll numbers would begin with a certain number) would be picked at random. For every mistake found, we would get a negative of 2 marks. In class, if a mobile would ring, the whole row of students would get minus 5 marks. Late arrival to class – minus 7 marks. People who would end up with a cumulative score of 0 at the end of the course would become demi-Gods. Minus 5 was reasonable. As long as you were not failing in the course, everything was acceptable. Prof Amar would give us sleepless nights, literally. The deadline for submitting his assignments would be 8 am and the whole college would be awake through the night.

Because of this lack of sleep, some brave-hearts would try to catch up sleep during other courses. Prof Akbar would teach Compensation Management. Akbar was the king of sarcasm. He used to kill with his puns (without you realizing that you have been shot at). One of my friends, Tiger Chakraborty (he was re-named by us after the Royal Bengal tiger), was trying to catch up on sleep during those classes. However, Tiger had a very witty knack of asking random questions during the class

[53] Maximum students would get martyred in this course

so that the Profs would think he was paying attention. This was termed as DCP (Desperate Class Participation). Thankfully, there were no extra points for DCP in most courses, else Tiger would have won the Sir Arnab Go-Tommy award for desperate attempts at academic excellence. Poor guy used to struggle a lot, but his CGPA was a miserable 5. That was Tiger, high on effort but miserable in terms of results. An inspired Tiger, in Prof Akbar's compensation class, asked a seemingly intelligent question "Professor, why is there so much disparity in the compensation between top management executives and the lower hierarchy? Don't you think the salary multiples are way too high?" Prof Akbar replied with uber-cool swag "My friend, that's a very intelligent question. What's your name?" Tiger was beaming with joy, having earned some much-needed brownie points. Tiger answered his name proudly and loudly. Prof Akbar said, "Very high energy, my friend. I like your question. But I had explained the answer to this when you had just started to doze off…" The whole class was in splits. After that Tiger never bothered to ask any questions in any class throughout XL.

The killer blow for me, though, came in Prof Anthony's class. Prof Anthony used to adopt a case study approach. It was the first time all of us were experiencing the famed case-based pedagogy. In each class, a group of four to five members would present their understanding of a case along with recommendations for solving the problem. In one of the case discussions, my friend Vivek was presenting the recommendations regarding how to deal with a manager, who had made a mistake which had cost the organization, but put the blame on his sub-ordinate. Prof. Anthony kept asking Vivek a lot of questions. There was one question though, which Vivek could not answer.

Prof: “Vivek, why did you think the manager did this? What could be the reason for putting the blame on the sub-ordinate?”

Vivek: “I am not sure, sir”

Prof: “Come on, try putting yourself in the manager’s shoes”

Vivek: “Sure sir. . . let me put myself in his shoes. . . give me a minute, sir”

I thought Vivek was going to remove his shoes, literally.

After a couple of seconds, Vivek contemplated and said “Sir, I don’t know why someone would blame a subordinate for his own action. I just cannot think of a reason to this, sir”

Prof: “Try, Vivek. You will get the answer. It’s not that difficult. Should I give you a clue?”

Vivek: “Sure, Sir”

Prof: “The clue is related to a theory related to human psychology”

Vivek: “I am sorry, sir. I am not a psychology student. I really can’t think of the reason, sir”

The Prof was not going to let Vivek go without an answer. He said “Come on, Vivek, apply your mind. It’s not that difficult.”

Vivek was now getting frustrated that the Prof was not letting go. He just kept silent, looking down at his shoes.

Prof: “Vivek, one last time. Why do you think the manager did this?”

A desperate Vivek, who wanted to finish the grill, shouted "To save his ass, sir. He did this to save his ass!!"

The whole class, including Prof Anthony, couldn't stop laughing. Poor Vivek had tried his best but he had cracked under pressure.

The story did not stop there, though. In those days, everyone wanted to be socially cool by posting funny Facebook status messages. This was 2010 and it was just two years of Facebook coming in India, having wiped out Orkut.

I thought this whole incident made a funny story. So, I put this on my FB wall and tagged Vivek. My FB status read as follows:

In today's class,

Prof Anthony: "Vivek, why did the manager do this?"

Vivek: "To save his ass, sir... ass"

The whole class, including Prof Anthony, went "ROFLMAO"

For those don't know, ROFLMAO is an internet slang that stands for "Rolling on the Floor Laughing My Ass Off"

This status of mine on FB made me an instant celebrity on XL social media. The post got more than 500 likes, it was shared by multiple people multiple times, it went viral in our campus, all in a week's time. I was mighty pleased by this.

Abhishek, a friend of mine, shared this on his wall. He was friends with Professor Ramdev Baba. Baba-ji used to teach Leadership. He seemed to be a pretty cool prof, who was very active on FB. Baba-ji had commented on Abhishek's post saying, "this is hilarious." I had never interacted with Baba-ji earlier. Neither Abhishek nor I had, in the wildest of dreams, imagined the next sequence of events.

Two days later, Abhishek called me and said "Abey Hari, jaldi aa. Mujhe kuch discuss karna hai tere saath[54]." His voice sounded very nervous. I immediately rushed to his room and asked him. He showed me an email sent by Prof Anthony.

"Dear Abhishek, you have insulted me by taking my name and using it on social media and have irreparably damaged my reputation. I am hereby dismissing you from my course. I am not accepting you as a student. Please do not come for the rest of the classes."

Me and Abhishek looked at each other in shock. My first question to Abhishek was "Prof Anthony is not on Facebook. Most of our Professors are not. How could he have known? Has any student who hates us taken revenge on us?"

But Abhishek immediately retorted "Bhai, it would not be a student because *koi itna buddhu nahi hai ki*[55] he will drag my name into this. It was you who posted it, not me. Definitely not a student. *Kuch alag hi locha hai*[56]"

Abhishek was right. An XLer would not be so dumb to drag a third person in this. We decided to read Prof Anthony's email to Abhishek again. The email had a screenshot of Abhishek's Facebook share. We couldn't make much from the screenshot.

---

[54] Hey, Hari. Come fast. I need to discuss something with you.

[55] Nobody is so foolish

[56] There is some other angle to this

We read the mail again. We could not find any clues. However, something interesting caught our eye. There was a trail mail, from guess who… Prof Ramdev Baba.

Babaji ka thullu mil hi gaya tha aaakhir[57]

Babaji had sent Abhishek's screenshot to Prof Anthony and had just mentioned the subject line as "Too funny, professor." In the body of the mail were the following two words

"FYI; screenshot :) "

Me and Abhishek were shocked. Knowingly or unknowingly, Babaji had almost finished our MBA life at XL. Prof Anthony was known to be a strict and no-nonsense chap. As it stood, he was part of the famed "Amar-Akbar-Anthony" trio which was notorious for failing students. *Anthony saab key saath panga*[58]. We were doomed.

We immediately rushed to Babaji and asked "Sir, aapne kyun share kiya humara post?[59]" Babaji coolly replied "Dudes, I thought it was too funny so I thought I will share it with my fellow colleagues. What's the big deal?"

We requested Babaji to speak to Prof Anthony and get us out of this trouble. Babaji's words would carry a lot of weight. Abhishek had a good rapport with him. But that was not to be. Babaji immediately took a U-turn and said "Folks, I am out of this. It's between you and Prof Anthony. I cannot interfere in issues which are not related to my course. "

Me and Abhishek then went to Prof Anthony directly. Prof Anthony, however, was not willing to talk to us. As soon as he

[57] Finally, Babaji had screwed us

[58] Taking on Anthony sir

[59] Sir, why did you share our Facebook post?

saw Abhishek, he asked him "After all the damage has been done, why have you brought your friend along?"

I then explained everything, that it was me who had written, and Abhishek had just *shared* the post and there was no fault of his. I apologized to him. But Prof would not have anything. He said, curtly, "What you have done has caused great damage to my reputation. If this was not enough, your friend has promoted this by sharing. You guys are dismissed from the course. Please don't bother me. I am hurt."

We were crestfallen. We didn't know what to do. We felt miserable. A seemingly innocuous post had landed us into trouble. We thought Babaji was a psycho. Ultimately, we had only ourselves to blame. We asked another Prof, who was close to us, and he suggested that only the Dean can help in this matter. We got scared now. The Dean was rumored to be an even bigger *Hitler* than Prof Anthony. But we had no option. We decided to be honest with him. We went to his cabin and I narrated the entire story. Looking at Abhishek's role, the dean was amused. We thought he would give us a mouthful.

But to our surprise, he was pretty cool. He told us "Look guys, what you have done is wrong and you have caused great damage to Prof Anthony, and in turn, XLRI. It's time you control the damage. My suggestion is that you take off the post and apologize to the Prof in public on social media. This will assuage his concern. Send the screenshot of the apology to the Prof. Mark me in copy. I will intervene and close this matter." We thanked him and left.

Immediately, I went and put up an apology post on Facebook. It read "Prof Anthony, I am really sorry for my actions. I did not intend to hurt you, or bring you or our institution in disrepute by publishing such stuff on social media. Please accept my public apology and I promise that I will never post such content on social media." I tagged Abhishek in that post. I put this post, took a screenshot, and in seconds, I deleted this post as well as the earlier post which had landed me in trouble. Immediately, Himanshu, Shravan and a few other friends pinged me on FB "Bro, why are you over-reacting? It's not needed. It's just fun. . . *Itna senti mat ho bhai. . . Kya bhasad hai ye sab...*[60]"

I didn't know that I had so many live stalkers. I told them I will explain later. I immediately sent an apology mail with the relevant screenshots, marked the Dean, went to Prof Anthony and apologized. It took a week but finally he relented. He was happy with our *social apology.*

1st year at XL had ended on a *socially awkward* note. I sang to myself:

"Aey merey Zuckerberg ki aulaat

Mat kar social media mey soothiyap

Warna karna padega zindagi bhar paschattaap

In case anything silly you post, like or share

Ripped apart will you be threadbare

Speech is sliver, silence is gold

If you *Don't* follow this in social media, then you are clean bowled!!

Karne jaagoge agar social media mey gadhon waali baat

Toh kaatna padega dean key office ka chakkar kaat

Aey merey Zuckerberg ki aulaat[61]"

---

60 Why are you becoming so sentimental? What's happening?

61 O son of Zuckerberg.... If you behave like a fool on social media, you will end up making trips to Dean's office

7

GMD - The Summer of 2010

T*hat* incident with Prof Anthony made me go off social media for almost a year. My only activity on Facebook would be wishing friends "Happy Birthday". I was in a social media depression. My friends would goad me into becoming active, but I was once bitten, twice shy. The first year had ended on quite an eventful note for me. It was time for the next chapter in my life – the summer internship.

We were asked to report at the company headquarters in Mumbai on Monday, the 11th of April 2010. The first two days was a super-drab corporate induction which we slept through. Each of the speakers went on and on and exceeded their allotted time limits. What was supposed to end at 6 pm ended at 8 pm on both the days. I guess these so-called senior folks had found bakras[62], who would listen patiently to their boring talks. Each of them used the word "strategy" a trillion times in their talks. If the word strategy was a human being, it would have complained of harassment by the end of 2 days. Everyone talked about mission, vision, core values, non-core values, CSR, VCR ... The sh*t was never ending. It was like the company was all perfect and the best place to work for. I was wondering why this company was slotted on day 2. The best part was that all of us were only interested in our projects but that topic was never

[62] Scapegoats

talked about. Gyaan[63], Kilobytes of Gyaan, Mega-Bytes, Kilo-Watts. It was quite overpowering. By the end of 2 days, we were roasted like chicken. The only solace was that everyone in every company was given the same dose. This made us feel relieved. *Doosron key dukh mey hume sukh milta hai.* [64]

The company was a conglomerate, and therefore, we were told to report to the group company headquarters the next day. There were 16 of us – all bundled into a conference room on the 6th floor. That would be our nest for the next two months. We were told that each of us would be called by our project guides during the day to get a briefing. Alas, none of us were called. We were later told by the HR that all of them were busy with a senior management review and hence the no-show. 3 days out of 60 days gone. While most of us were patiently waiting, a mahaarathi[65] decided to take charge. He started watching YouTube videos with his headphones on. Whenever the HR coordinator would walk in, he would just switch the tab over to another YouTube window which had videos of the company chairman speaking. The HR praised him for "making effective use of available time". We were now jealous. The next day, all of us had got our earphones. We also went into YouTube mode.

Finally, on the Friday, I guess the company folks remembered us and called each of us one by one. I was slotted in the afternoon. I went to my guide. Her visiting card read "Priya Saxena, Senior GM – HR." She told me "Hari, the project which we have decided to give you is a very *critical* project for the company. We are very serious about this project and we expect the same from you." The next 45 minutes, she explained

---

[63] Knowledge

[64] We are happy to see others suffer, like us(a sense of fairness and relief)

[65] Special One

the project to me. In those 45 minutes, the word *critical* would have been used at least 1000 times to drive home the point. I narrated this to my friends in the 6th floor once I came back. Thanks to the project, I got a nickname "Critical" Hari.

In those days, getting a Pre-Placement Offer (PPO) was the single-minded aim of a B-school student doing a summer internship. A PPO, or *pappu,* would guarantee an exit from the placement process, which meant you could chill through the entire second year. *Saam-daan-dhand-bhed – kuch bhi karne key liye tayyar they*[66] . . . for Pappu. A few students would order lunch for their guides, some would get them sweets, some, if given an option, were ready to iron their clothes, wash their vessels. All this in the hope of getting brownie points from their guides. Some would deliberately sit late and close the office gate with the security guard just to show off their hard work. I used to sometimes wonder – what's the use of an MBA degree if ultimately all that takes to survive is boot-licking/ sycophancy. But before I could dwell deeper, my friends would break my thoughts and say "Abey Critical, jyaada critically mat soch. Joh likha hai, wahi hoga. Pappu milna hai toh milega[67]. Let's call it a day and go for dinner." I never used to understand why students had to resort to such under-arm bowling tactics to get a PPO. I was least bothered about all this. I explored Mumbai to the hilt. We used to stay in Wilson College hostel in South Mumbai. We explored every reasonable hotel in Chowpatty area, barring the 5-star ones, which were out of our budget. We watched an IPL semi-final, visited Haji Ali, Siddhivinayak Temple, watched a play. My birthday was celebrated in Essel World. On another weekend, we explored Kashid beach and the Janjira fort in

[66] We were willing to go to any lengths (hook-or-crook) to get a PPO

[67] Hey, Critical. What's destined to happen will happen. If PPO is written in your destiny, it will happen

Murud, the fort in the middle of the sea. Another weekend, we went to Shirdi. I started loving Mumbai. My stipend was 20,000 rupees but within 20k, I could manage all these. That's Mumbai for you – it teaches you to live and enjoy under any salary.

My project was titled "Integrated Employee Engagement Strategy". It felt like the guide liked these 4 words in her B school days and decided to join them and make a project out of it. There were 3 survey dumps given to me – one was an internal survey, the other was by an agency called "Wallop" and the third by an organization called FPTW (Fake Place to Work). Each of them had 200 questions. I had to arrive at a common theme and give my recommendations on how to go ahead. I wondered "Ajeeb siyaapa hai BC[68]." Why do 3 surveys, why spend extra money, why get confused and then why correlate them? If you want to know the employee pulse, can't a simple survey followed by Focus Group Discussions (FGDs) and talking to your employees be enough? I asked this to my guide. She said "When I was young like you, I also used to wonder. Don't worry. You will find the answers yourself as you get sucked into the corporate world." After that, I stopped asking questions to my guide. It was time for my mid-project presentation. I presented my analysis in a PowerPoint Presentation, in bullet points. I thought I had done a great job of the analysis. I thought my guide would sing "Taareef karoon kya uski… jisne tumhe banaya[69]."

Instead, I got a huge dressing down from my guide "XL sey aaye ho[70].. Don't you know how to present something? Where are the smart-arts? Where are the animations? Where are the

---

[68] How stupid

[69] Praises to the One who created me

[70] You have come from XL

flow-charts? Look at the font- Times New Roman. Couldn't you have used a creative font like Century Gothic? Important keywords to be highlighted in bold. There are no fancy graphs. This is very straight-forward and simple. I don't see any effort in this presentation. All you have done is analyzd excel sheets, which anyone can do. Where is the B school flavor? Hari, this is a "critical" project but you are not taking this seriously. You seriously need to work on your presentation skills."

I wondered "Ek toh 3 random surveys ka analysis aur co-relation karna hi itna tough tha[71]. I somehow found a way and got some meaning into this random project. Instead of appreciating my effort, I am being ripped apart for font size, smart art, animations?" I thought that was not my job; the analysis is the difficult part. Lesson learnt. "Jo dikhta hai, wo bikta hai[72]."

My friend, who had spent half the time I had spent on the project, but made a good visual presentation came out smiling "Bhai, mazaa aa gaya. Meri PPT ki taareef hi taareef… kaabil-e-taareef… Tum gadhey ho... Tumhare analysis apne paas rakho aur dikhaawe pey lag jao. Clear hai?[73]"

I had learnt the importance of a visually appealing PPT the hard way. But better late than ever. After my mid-project review, I decided to work on my PPT skills. Every evening, I would practice animations and smart art. By the end of two weeks, this is how my slide would look. An arrow would start from the left corner of the screen, swirl in circular motion, and finally

---

[71] I had done a tough job of drawing correlation from 3 random surveys

[72] Presentation is important for anything to sell

[73] Bro, I had great fun. My PPT got a lot of praise. You are a fool. Keep your analysis aside and focus on the visual presentation. Is it clear?

become a square and settle at the right corner of the screen. I felt this was it. I had conquered Everest.

I made a 60-slide final presentation. The first slide was my favorite slide. On the first click, the words "Integrated Employee Engagement Analysis – Summer Project Presentation" would appear from the left to the right. On the next click, these words would spin like Shaktimaan[74] for 30 seconds and then they would disappear and the following words would enter from the middle of the screen and enlarge like a Yash Raj film logo "R… Hari. . . Hara. . . Subramanian…. XLRI. . . 2011. . . HR" I had shown a draft presentation with this slide to my guide and she was impressed *"Ye hui na XL waali baat… Sota hua sher jaag utha… Bahut Badhiya[75]"*

The D-day (the final presentation round) was drawing close. We were all excited and nervous. The organization had taken 70 interns across businesses, functions, and the top 3 would get a PPO. Each business and function would nominate the top 2 interns and the final 10 would battle it out. Since in our HR function, we were only 3 interns, 1 would get eliminated. The dates were announced- Monday, June 5th was the presentation round 1. Those who made the cut would do another presentation on June 6th, and the awards for the top 3 would be presented on June 7th in front of everyone.

I was reasonably confident about my chances. My guide was pretty impressed with my work and since she was in the panel with two other senior leaders, I was sure she would recommend me for the next round. I also had animations in 55 out of my

[74] Popular Indian TV series of the 90s where the lead character would swivel in the air and save people

[75] Wow. This looks like a PPT with an "XL" stamp. The sleepy lion has woken and is now roaring.

60 slides. The slides which didn't have animations had great visuals. I also had an inspirational quote in the last slide.

The D-day arrived, the 5th of June 2010. I had made 3 dry runs and timed it under 30 minutes. We waited eagerly for our presentation slot. The first to go were the sales and marketing folks. 10 of them, then the 3 finance folks. It was 5 pm, and next were the 3 HR interns. We waited and waited. Nothing happened. I went and asked the HR coordinator. She said they are waiting for the panelists to arrive. We waited for another 2 hours. Nothing happened. We continued to wait in the hope that the presentation would start late. But the HR coordinator also went absconding. We tried reaching her mobile but it was not reachable. We didn't know what to do. We had no option but to wait. We waited till 9 pm. The security guard came in and told us to leave. Meanwhile, the HR coordinator sent an SMS to all of us saying 2 folks from Sales & Marketing and 1 from Finance had made it to the final round. There was no news about the HR interns.

We came back the next day. The second round had started. HR interns from other group companies had been shortlisted, including my HR friend Siddharth. I couldn't understand what was going on. It was lunch and round 2 presentations were done. I asked our HR coordinator but she also had no clue. She, however, told us that round 2 was over and since our names were not nominated, we would not be going through.

I went to my guide and asked her what happened. She replied "Hari, I am extremely sorry. Me and the other two panelists could not agree on a common time slot yesterday to judge your presentations. I was not free in the second half while the other two were not free in the first half. We had a lunch meeting with the CEO so we couldn't do it."

I prodded, "But couldn't you have called us early morning today or maybe a bit later at a coffee shop? At least we would have got a fair chance? Don't you think so?"

She said "I know you are getting emotional but nothing can be done now."

I asked her "Couldn't you have just given 2 names out of the 3. At least someone from us would have gotten a shot. You had all 3 presentations with you on your laptop?"

She said "It's against my ethics, Hari"

I thought to myself "Waah mere HR waali mata. Presentation nahi dekha aur pappu ka sapna toda, wahaan ethics yaad nahi aaya[76]"

My friend Siddharth won the Best presentation award and got the PPO. We told him our story and he couldn't stop laughing. Wednesday, June 7th, at the awards night, the Group President was interacting with us. He asked me over drinks "How was your overall internship experience?"

I slowly muttered "Fuck all, sir"

He seemed to have heard it. He asked me "Did I hear you say something?" I immediately gathered my wits and said "Brinjal sir, brinjal... I am admiring the brinjal in today's buffet. The baingan[77] is really good. The whole internship experience, including today's event, is world class, Sir. I will never forget my final presentation, sir, as I got some really nice feedback from my HR mentors."

---

[76] Oh, HR Goddess! Where did your ethics disappear when you didn't even bother to see my presentation? You have broken my dream of getting a PPO.

[77] Brinjal

With a beaming smile, which could have been used in Close-up toothpaste ads, he left with a few parting words "Son, life is all about ups and downs. You did your best, unfortunately you didn't win a PPO. This doesn't mean you are any less than the winner. It's about the journey, not the destination. All the best."

At that moment, I couldn't help remembering the famous song GMD (Gaa*d Mein Danda) sung by Bodhi Tree, our college band.

"Guide tha uska bada haraami.
Pappu ka toda sapna
2nd year mey waapis aa gaya.
Haath mey lekar apna
Gaa*d pey pad gayi laaat.
Aur toota sapno ka mahal
Teri Gaa*d mey Danda rey,
Teri Gaa*d mey Danda rey
Na Baans ki Bansi, Na Sone ka Sariya,
Gaa*d mey Danda rey[78]"

[78] His Guide was a sly fox. He screwed his chances of a PPO. He had to come back to second year empty-handed. A rod had been shoved up his ass

8

Lord Hari Ki Jai

After a fruitless summer internship, it was back to the grind in second year. As the PPO had eluded me, I had to do the hard work in second year – ensure grades were decent, build some CV points, get elected in one of the clubs. All this to get a decent placement. It was a tough ask but there was a silver lining. All my group of Bakchod[79] friends had missed the PPO. There were 8 of us in our core group – nobody had gotten a PPO. The thought of not being alone was a big motivator. *Doobenge toh sab saath mey*[80]. One fine evening, on the 26th of June 2010, my friend Himanshu Joshi randomly dared me that he would make me the Lord of XL – Lord Hari. I laughed at him and said there's no way this can happen. I am not going to take any sh*t on me. I dared him – "Dum hai to kar key dikha[81]." That was it. Joshi was the head of Cowbaxi (the Cow belt association of XLRI). It was not easy to become the head of the Northern/Central states (UP, Bihar, Madhya Pradesh, etc.) Joshi decided to show why he was called Bahubali[82]. That same day, he went door to door and started collecting chanda[83] from each of the hostel folks. His pitch was "Aaj Lord ka naamkaran

---

[79] Person who talks a lot of crap or does exaggerated talks

[80] We will all go down together

[81] If you have the guts, do it and show me

[82] The Ultimate Warrior

[83] Donation

hai[84]. Please contribute. And you are invited for it." I had no clue about the things to follow. People actually started contributing chanda. A sum of 361 rupees was collected. Joshi and Gaurav Jain went to the nearby market and bought samagris[85] – Dhoop, Chandan, Kumkum, a puja-bell (ghanta) and a sweet box. I was curious and asked Joshi "bhaiyaa sweets kis liye hai?" He retorted "Lord ka bhog chadne waala hai[86]." I was getting confused. This lord sh*t was for real. Vinay Poojary, my creative friend, had designed a poster and emailed it to the batch "Gather at 9:30 pm in first floor for the Lord's coronation. You don't want to miss this!!"

I had no clue what was happening around me. People now were actually getting excited. They started assembling near the open area towards the first floor. Himanshu Joshi was shocked. What started as a prank suddenly became an event with high turnout. Joshi immediately convened a quick core committee meeting- Joshi, Poojary and Gaurav Jain. Joshi instructed "Gaurav – tum hawan ka intezaam karo. Ishita aur Gauri ko bulao – woh log gaana gayenge. Poojary – tum Tiger aur gang ko bolo ki fourth floor khaali karen aur sab ko first floor open area mey bulayen. Rohan and team Hari ko tayyar karenge. Ek dum baba waala look aana chahiye. Main crowd ko control karoonga[87]." Things started to move quickly.

People started innovatively contributing. Tiger, Rohan Raghunath, and 4 other henchmen literally sedated me.

---

[84] Today is Lord's naming ceremony

[85] Prayer essentials

[86] Me- "Man, why have you brought sweets?" Joshi- "Sweets in honour of the Lord"

[87] Gaurav, you arrange for the pyre. Call up Ishita and Gauri – they will sing the song. Poojary- inform Tiger and Gang to vacate the 4th floor and ensure people assemble in the first floor. I will control the crowd.

They made me remove my shirt. The chalk powder became a vibhooti[88] and was promptly applied on my face. From nowhere, a veshti[89] appeared and I was told to remove my jeans. I tried to run away but Rohan removed my jeans at gunpoint and made me tie the veshti. This was for real. I had no choice. Tiger, meanwhile, arranged an umbrella. The script was made. I would come from the fourth floor, all the way down with chants of "Lord Hari Ki Jai". Vinay and Souvik arranged for a few rogues who would chant "Lord Hari ki Jai" as soon as I would start coming down. The stage was set. I had never been subjected to such random ragging in my life.

Meanwhile, the crowd at the first floor was getting restless. Joshi was yelling in his mike "Bhaiyon aur behenon, agle bees minute mey Lord upar sey padhaarne waale hain[90]." The mob was getting restless. They started walking towards the fourth floor. I was locked in a room with Rohan and Tiger. Rohan said "Hilne ka nai[91] ... Until we will tell you, you will not come out" I was getting frustrated, not knowing what to do. Amrit Jami, our law expert friend, started writing something on a paper. When asked, he said "The Lordship Act." Everyone had gone crazy, except me. One of my friends, Nattu, showed sympathy on me and protested to Himanshu and group that I should not be insulted this way. Rohan immediately interjected "Kisi ne bhi ungli kiya, toh unka Lord banaya jaayega[92] instead of Hari. Are you ok?" That was enough to silence my well-wishers.

---

[88] Religious powder which is applied on forehead

[89] Traditional Tamil cloth, used instead of a trouser

[90] Brothers and sisters, the Lord will come down in another 20 mins

[91] Don't move

[92] If anybody points a finger at this activity, he will be declared as the Lord instead of Hari

Meanwhile, the crowd was getting restless. It was time for action. Himanshu Joshi screamed in the mic "Mitron. . . Lord Hari. . . 4th floor sey padhaarne waale hain !![93]" As if it was a miracle, a drum came out of nowhere and Sreekanth Madipathi started beating the drums. The music started. People had done on-the-spot innovation to make it a larger-than-life event. The drumbeats started getting louder. Somebody opened the door of our room. I was reluctant to go. I tried putting a fight but Rohan pushed me out. I wanted to cry but there I saw a mob of 150 cheering and clapping as soon as I had come out. There were huge chants of "Lord Hari Ki Jai[94]". Behind me came Tiger with an umbrella. Suddenly, Rohan gave me chalk powder and asked me to throw it on the crowd.

I wanted to protest but there was no way out. I didn't want to make it an anti-climax to all those people who had patiently waited for an hour in anticipation. So, I decided to play to the gallery. I threw the powder in all four directions. I was asked to walk slowly. I had to take at least 30 minutes to walk all the floors. People were falling at my feet "Lord, aashirwad dijiye. Prabhu, humari maange poori kijiye[95]." Rohan immediately signalled me to bless the bhakts[96]. I gave a scornful look but he said "If you don't do it, we will make you, which will not look good." So, I started blessing people. Some people came and tried touching my feet. Himanshu and team shooed them away. The crowd was going berserk. We had walked for about two floors and the vibhuti was out. I had to walk for two more floors. Someone gave me a bunch of guavas. I was flabbergasted. Don't tell me that I had to throw guavas at the crowd. Joshi whispered in my

---

[93] Friends, Lord Hari is going to come down from the 4th floor

[94] All Hail Lord Hari

[95] Lord, bless us. Fulfil our wishes

[96] Devotees

ear "Abey janta key high expectations hai. Jo bhi haath mey diya, bas phekta jaa... Baaki hum sambhaal lenge[97]." So, Lord Hari started throwing guavas as gifts to the bhakts. We walked slowly amidst drumbeats, bhajans and chants of "Lord Hari Ki Jai" and finally reached the first-floor open area.

I thought the ordeal had ended. But no, the best was yet to come. There was a *hawan*[98] which was lit up. We reached the hawan. Himanshu again yelled at the mic "Bhakton, abhi Lord ki aarti utaṛi jaayegi[99]." The mike was handed over to Ishita. Eponymously, Aarti, my classmate, started doing the aarti. Ishita started singing "Om Jai Jagdish hare. . ." The crowd joined in the chorus. Sreekanth was ferociously drumming away. It was like Shivamani meeting Anup Jalota and performing devotional fusion, with bhakts adding to the background noise. Then, they started washing my feet. My friend *Bhai* got so emotionally involved that he drank the water from my feet. This was getting crazier.

I thought that the event was done with my feet being washed. But like Bhai, Ishita had gotten seriously into the character. She furiously screamed at Himanshu "How can you let him go without me reciting all the slokas?" Me and Himanshu looked at each other. We were not expecting this. Himanshu winked at me and said "Bilkul[100], Ishita. Let us do a proper ceremony." So, after 20 minutes of Ishita's bhajans and pooja, where drops of water were sprinkled in the hawan, the mayhem stopped. I was escorted to my room. I was relieved.

---

[97] Brother, the crowd is having high expectations. Throw whatever we are giving you, towards the crowd. We will manage the rest.

[98] Pyre

[99] Devotees, we will have an aarti (prayer with lamp) for the Lord

[100] Absolutely

But Himanshu had other plans. He announced "Now, we will have the *ghanta*[101] installation ceremony in Lord's abode." I suddenly looked above the door outside my room. A ghanta had been installed. It was getting worse. I was told to ring the bell once. Ishita again interjected "Joshi ji, its 3 times as per Ved Shastra." I wanted to give a piece of my mind to her but before I knew, the drumbeats started getting louder. So, I rang the ghanta 3 times and entered the room. There were huge claps all around. Sweets were getting distributed. I thought I was done for the day, but it was not to be. I was told to sit like Lord Vishnu in the Govinda Raja Swamy avatar. I had to face sideways with my head wresting on my hands. The placement committee folks came in from nowhere and said, "Lord, please bless us for the placements." I wanted to say "Screw you, fuckers", but after my PPO disaster, I changed my mind and said, with a beaming smile- "Bhagwan aap key saath hai[102]."

Himanshu yelled at the mic "Lord Hari ne placement team ko aashirwaad dey diya doston. Ab humara 100 placement pakka[103]" There was a huge roar from the crowd, which reminded me of Eden Gardens[104] roaring for a Sourav Ganguly boundary. Looking at the Placement committee, the Student Affairs Committee (SAC) members, I guess, got jealous. They came next and said "Lord, aapne Placecom ko blessings de diya[105]. What about us?" I wanted to reply "Abey gadhon…Tum soothiya,tumhara placecom soothiya… Sab

---

[101] Bell

[102] The Lord is with you

[103] Friends, the Lord has blessed the placement team. Now, we are sure of 100% placements

[104] Cricket stadium in Kolkata

[105] Lord, you have blessed the Placecom

soothiye hain[106]" But I decided not to spoil a great show and said "Bhagwan SAC key saath hai[107]." Himanshu again shouted. "Mitron, Lord ney SAC ko bhi apna aashirwad dey diya hai[108]" Huge applause followed by chants of "Lord Hari Ki Jai". For the next 45 minutes, every club on campus came with their secretary and took their blessings. I was tired and exhausted now. It was a 2-hour extravaganza and none of it was planned. Himanshu joshi schemingly laughed "Beta, Bahubali sey panga lega na... toh yehi hoga[109]." I literally pleaded him to end this event. Finally, after all the prasad was distributed (30 sweet boxes had been miraculously procured), everyone went home.

Lord Hari made me a celebrity on campus. The second year, I badly wanted to get into a campus club as I had got rejected in all the clubs in my first-year interviews by my seniors. Thankfully, there were no interviews in second year for club membership. It was an election and the folks with the highest votes would enter the clubs. I stood for the Industrial Relations Club (FIRE-@X) and rattled off a speech. I was pitted against some strong candidates, including some existing club members, who were sure to get re-elected. But I guess Lord Hari had swelled my campus popularity. The results were announced, and I got the highest votes, even crossing the existing club members. Himanshu Joshi did not stop at Lord Hari. The juniors were told to elect their own Lord and before graduation, a Lord handover ceremony was conducted with me handing over the crown to Lord Vinayak.

---

106 You fools. Each of you, including the Placecom are idiots.

107 Lord is with SAC

108 Friends, Lord has given his blessings to SAC as well

109 Mate, if you mess with Bahubali, this is what will end up happening

Lord Vinayak handed it over to Lord Gopa Kumar and the tradition continued for a few years.

It has been more than 10 years since "Lord Hari Ki Jai" but after that incident, I have never dared anyone with the lines "Dum hai toh karke dikha[110]", courtesy Himanshu Joshi ki Jai[111].

[110] Dare to do it

[111] Hail Himanshu Joshi

9

Mom N Me

While Lord Hari got me elected to the Industrial Relations club, it also had its share of disadvantages. Post every birthday, I would be given birthday bumps[112] by my batchmates for being the Lord. This also was Himanshu Joshi's brainchild. To teach him a lesson, I started eating food at Dadu's, our in-house food station, and would tell Dadu to put all my bills in Himanshu Joshi's account. Joshi had a running credit account. One day, Himanshu got the shock of his life when he saw 3 burgers, 6 samosas and 4 teas written against his name when he was away from campus. Until then, I had neatly debited him with about 1000 rupees. Post that, Himanshu moved from post-paid billing to cash on consumption. But the damage had been done.

Having become a member of the Industrial Relations Club, my next task at hand was to win a case study contest so that I could "build" my CV. CV building in second year had more benefits to a B school student's health, than body building. I had to tick all the boxes in my CV to get a decent job and ensure I recover the 10 plus lacs invested for my two- year course. Winning case study competitions was a big CV point.

[112] Being kicked on your buttocks by a group of people

WIMC (Well-Known Indian Management Conglomerate, pronounced as "Wim-cee") was one of the biggest names on campus. In those days, there was a competition called WIMC War Room. It was the biggest B school competition in those days, with the winning team from campus getting to participate in the Grand Finale in Mumbai and getting to interact with the Chairman. He was one of the biggest names in Indian industry and the chance of meeting him was a big motivator to participate in the case study competition. Shravan, Manan, Yashowardhan, and me, registered for the WIMC War Room. We were determined to ace the competition. WIMC was a conglomerate with different industry verticals. Each industry had a case study challenge and we were allowed to choose the industry of our choice and submit our solution to the case. We were fascinated by the retail sector. WIMC had a brand called "Mom & Me", a chain of stores for -9 to +9 (pregnant ladies and kids). The case study challenge for "Mom & Me" was to find out the current operational challenges being faced in the stores by conducting primary research in a city of our choice, and suggest a city store strategy for winning in the retail market in India along with an international market entry strategy. Again, like in the case of my summer internship project title, the word "strategy" arrived to screw my happiness. If "strategy" were a human being, it would have been filed under 36 million cases per day of harassment, substance abuse, attempt to murder, humiliation, and felony. In the hope of creating history by winning a case study competition for the first time ever, the four of us decided to name our team as "History Makers".

As me and Shravan were from Hyderabad, Manan was from Bhilai, and Yash, (fondly called "Yosha") from Lucknow, we decided to pick Hyderabad as the city of survey. During our term break, we decided to do our research work in Hyderabad.

In Himayatnagar area, there was a "Mom N Me" store. The stores were supposed to have a premium feel as they catered to a very niche upper middle-class audience. This Himayatnagar store was nowhere close to premium. The entrance was dimly lit. We walked in on a Saturday afternoon but the store was empty. The receptionist had a grumpy look on her face as though she had not had food for the past thirty days. We first thought we will do a mystery survey as consumers, but none of us looked anyway close to a dad or having kids. The closest resemblance to being a dad was Yosha, but he was not with us. So, we decided to chuck the idea. We told the receptionist that we were students from XLRI and had come on a project work.

"XLRI? What is that?" was the receptionist's response. We told her that it was one of the top B schools in the country. "What is B school, sir?" was her next query. At that moment, a senior person, who was overhearing our conversation from the corner of the store walked in toward us and asked us "Aap log IIM sey ho[113]?" We said "No, sir, we are from XLRI." He immediately asked "XLRI, what is that?" Shravan and I looked at each other. People knew the word IIM, but not XLRI. What a sad feeling, although XLRI was considered to be better than half of the IIMs (In those days, there were 6 IIMs – BLACKI[114] and XL was at par with IIM C, and above L, I and K in terms of overall rankings). We replied, "It is amongst the top 5 B schools, at par with the IIMs." The conversation continued and we asked the manager all sorts of questions – store footfalls, profitability, manpower challenges. The manager let out all his frustration with his superiors to us "Sir, yahaan A/C theek karane key liye bhi boss ka permission lagta hai, sir. Attrition

[113] Are you from the IIMs (Indian Institutes of Management)

[114] Bangalore, Lucknow, Ahmedabad, Calcutta, Kozhikode & Indore

bahut hai, sir[115]. They don't pay salaries on time, sir. Big boss bahut bada baniya hain[116]. Customer walk-ins are good but most of the time, we don't order the right stocks, so customers are not offered products of their choice. Plus, there is lot of favoritism, sir. In case you know of any openings, please let me know. I will give my card to you. You can come here for the next 20 days whenever you want and do all your research. I will also arrange for a few customer interviews so that you can enquire about the overall experience."

We felt sad for the store manager. We initially thought the store manager had a bad experience and he was unnecessarily biased. Mom & Me was a respected brand managed by one of the most respected business houses in the country, and it surely could not have been managed this badly. We interviewed a few other sales reps but the story was no different. After spending close to 10 days in the store, we decided to wind up our primary research and start working on our presentation.

Our recommendations were hard-hitting, at least we thought so. We recommended a complete operational overhaul of Mom & Me, right from the store layout, lighting, receptionist behavior, staff motivation, along with other marketing related recommendations like having a brand ambassador like Aishwarya Rai Bachchan, who had just got pregnant at that time. We put a lot of photographs of the store visit to lend credibility to our recommendations. Manan was our PPT expert. Like how a typical Bollywood movie is incomplete without an item number, no PPT is complete without graphic animations. So, we put up an image of a Humpty Dumpty

[115] Sir, you need to take permission of the boss for repairing the AC. There is high attrition here sir.

[116] The big boss is a miser

egg shell with a thumbs up to indicate "what's working with Mom & Me". Humpty Dumpty with thumbs down indicated "what's not working". This was Yosha's creative idea. Having sexed up the presentation with slide transitions, smart arts, and animations, we sent our submission and prayed that we would get shortlisted.

9 teams were shortlisted for the presentation round and the last name announced was "History Makers". We were elated. We were confident of creating history. Manan and I rehearsed the presentation while Shravan and Yosha timed us and gave feedback. As a group, we decided that the best presenters would present. Me and Manan were suited up. We spent about 500 bucks each to get a facial done so that we could impress the judges with our "executive presence".

The 9 teams were asked to assemble at 6 pm sharp for the presentation round. We were all excited. We were just a presentation away from meeting the chairman of WIMC. We were confident of our work. Manan was already dreaming about visiting the headquarters of WIMC in Worli, Mumbai. We also dreamt of getting the War Room Trophy to XLRI.

3 hours passed by and there was no sign of the jury. The senior management of WIMC were supposed to judge all our presentations and short-list the winner. Finally, at 10:30 pm, two gentlemen in blazers turned up. Manan and I were super excited. Here was our chance to create history. The team's name "History Makers" was so apt. One gentleman from WIMC walked up and started his announcement.

"Folks, we apologize for the delay in turning up. On our way from Ranchi, there was a huge traffic jam on the highway. It was not expected. We, at WIMC, are extremely happy with the quality of presentations received. However, in the interest of time, we have a small request. If all of you agree, we can implement this…"

We were confused. These two folks had come almost 5 hours late and on top of this, another twist in the tale. The gentleman continued "Friends, all the 9 entries are really good. But if we see all 9 entries and assume 30 minutes for each presentation, we are looking at close to 5 hours from now and we will end up at 4 am and we have to leave by 6 am. So, here is what I propose…

We will see the top 6 presentations and select the winner. All 9 submissions will, however, get the campus round finalist certificate though. This is just to save time. We will only do this if it's ok with all of you. Please discuss. I will step out for 5 minutes and hear from all the teams"

This was not what we were expecting. 3 teams, despite being shortlisted, would miss out. What if we were amongst those unlucky 3? We thought we will oppose the idea. All the 9 teams got into a huddle. One of our friends proposed that all 9 teams should be allowed to present, as we all had sweated it out and it would be unfair on the 3 teams missing out. It was the WIMC folks' mistake of not being on time and it was their headache if they get only two hours to sleep. Most of us seemed to agree, but then the Placement Committee member (Place-com) interrupted "Guys, let's not get emotional. If the WIMC folks want to only look at 6 entries, let's go with their suggestion. They are a big company and they may pick up more than 5 students in final placements if we support them. Participation certificate is anyway being given for the last 3. And these teams are not the first 6, so anyways, its fair justice." Place-com in B schools is more powerful than the Prime Minister of any country. Even the PM can't influence Place-com. So, we went with the concept of "fair justice" as suggested by our Lord Ram from Place-com. The 6 names were announced, and our name was not there. So much so for the "History Makers". My bad luck had come to haunt me again. The same bad luck which screwed me in the BM interview and cost me my summer internship PPO. "Paandu Kismat[117]"

Manan and I removed our blazers in frustration and decided to not see the other presentations. But Shravan and Yash convinced us not to get too emotional. Yash used his favorite one-liner "When life hands you lemons... DEMAND tequila and Salt! Piyenge BC[118]" Sukh mey daaru, dukh mey bhi daaru[119]. No wonder Kingfisher sells like hot cakes in our country. Shravan, who was a tee-totaller in those days, stopped all of us and said "Let us look at the other presentations. At least we will get an idea why we failed to make it." It made sense. So, we sat through the 6 presentations, but we had no clue as to why we had failed to make the cut. The other presentations were equally good or bad as ours, whichever way we looked at. We had sweated ourselves by conducting primary research, sitting in the "Mom & Me" store, but all this to no avail. Our chance of manufacturing a great CV point went up in smoke.

They say every cloud has a silver lining. I have never been able to spot the silver line in any cloud till date. To me, clouds have always been black (Kaale Baadal). Disappointed, we walked back. However, we earned a lot of respect in our batch for making it to the campus final of WIMC War Room. We were told that 45 entries were submitted and only 9 made it

[117] Rotten Luck

[118] We will drink

[119] Drink when happy, drink when sad

to the final round. On our walk back from the auditorium to our room, a couple of good-looking girls, who had never ever spoken to us, came and congratulated us for making it to the final round. Yash was over the moon. "Bhai, Madam ney humse haath milaya bhai. Dil khush ho gaya bhai[120]". Manan also suddenly had a Colgate smile when a girl came and gave him a hand-shake. We had found our silver lining.

A few months later, WIMC came to our campus for lateral placements. They shortlisted me and congratulated me for making it to the final round of War Room. I got through WIMC and signed out of the placement process. That was the silver lining for me. WIMC War Room had made each of us happy for different reasons. For Manan and Yash, it was the girls congratulating, for me it was landing a job. We were not completely able to comprehend Shravan's happiness, though. Seeing all 3 of us happy, probably he also was very happy. Plus, he became a sought-after project guy amongst the girls. He did not get an internship PPO, but instead received a lot of PPOs (Pre-Project Offers) from girls "Hey Shravan, can I be part of your project team? Hi Shravan, next project, I am in your team, ok?" We did not win WIMC War Room but we had taken a small step in our dream to become "Campus Studs".

At the WIMC induction, I met a senior, Aditya Vaidya, who had joined WIMC from MDI Gurgaon a year ago and was working for "Mom & Me". I took him offline and told him about the sad state of affairs in the store in Himayatnagar. I asked him- "Why aren't you doing something about this store, Aditya? The store manager's and the team's morale are low. Incentives

[120] Bro, this girl has given me a handshake, which I never dreamt of. I am elated

nahi milta[121]. The lighting is poor. The store sucks. It pains me. " Before I could get further emotional, Aditya stopped me "Dude, how can it be possible? We don't have a store in Himayatnagar. I am pretty sure." I told him "Bhai, tumhe tumhare stores nahi pata hai kya?[122]. It must have been newly opened." Aditya retorted "Dude, shut up. Don't teach me about my business." I showed him the store photos on my phone. He started laughing loudly. I couldn't understand. I was angry. I told him "Dude, we worked our ass off and you are mocking us. How shameful and disgusting!!!" Aditya couldn't control his laughter. He said "Dude, please don't talk about this project to anyone in this company again. The store you have visited is Mom "N" Me. Our brand is Mom "&" Me. You have visited some cheap duplicate store and done your project. Look carefully." He was right. In our excitement, we had not looked at the store's name-board. It was Mom "N" Me. I immediately called the other History Makers. Yash was the one laughing the loudest. He again quoted his famous Lemons and Tequila quote, and said "Let's head out. Aaj ki shaam, Mom "N" Me key naam. Piyo BC[123]"

---

121 Incentives are not being given

122 Bro, don't you know where your stores are located?

123 Tonight, we will drink in memory of "Mom N Me"

10

Andhra meals

After a highly eventful fourth trimester – which started with Lord Hari and culminated with Mom N Me, we moved to the fifth. The fifth term at XL was dominated by regional club dinners. Every club would get to host a cultural night – dinner for the whole college followed by cultural performances. Being a Hyderabadi, I was part of APAXI (Andhra Pradesh Association of XLRI). Everyone was part of some or the other regional club based on their place of origin and native language. As I was a Tam-brahm[124], I also was part of TAXI (Tamil Nadu Association of XLRI). By some random tradition, ROBAXI (Royal Bengal Association at XLRI) would always start first and COWBAXI, the cow belt, would end it. In those todays, Telangana was not yet declared as a separate state, so Andhra Pradesh had a single regional club.

The cultural performances were a chance for people to show off their varied talents – singing, dancing, skit, mimicry etc. I was told by the APAXI dance team that I would be part of a legendary dance. I agreed, thinking we would be dancing away to Hrithik's 'Ek Pal Ka Jeena'. Wishful thinking! Instead, me, Sreekanth Madhipati and Dinakar Bonda danced to a Telugu song called "Yankamma". For those who don't know Telugu, Yankamma translates to "Nimmajji" in Kannada and "Teri Maa

[124] Tamil Brahmin

Ki" in Hindi. I was told it would be a towel dance. I thought I would be grooving away like Bhai in the song 'Jeene Ke Hai Chaar Din'. Wishful thinking again!! I ended up wearing a towel on my head and dancing the whole song with a towel on my head. Madhipati and Bonda danced like Bhai and Hrithik. I was made to throw the towel into the crowd at the end of the dance. I still have that towel with me. Somebody, when I become a celebrity writer and years later, when they decide to auction some of my priceless belongings at Sotheby's or Christy's, I am sure the towel will fetch quite a bomb.

The explosion though, was reserved for the dinner. In one of the organizing committee meets for the APAXI dinner (There were only 12 members from AP. Therefore, everyone decided to call everyone organizers), Sandeep Mekala, proposed that we should do something innovative and show why APAXI is different from the crowd. We were not sure what innovation one could bring out in a regional dinner. All that was required was to hire a caterer, inform the quantity and serve the cooked food which would be brought in containers. There was the catch. Mekala said, "Let's change the game. Let's get the food cooked in campus. Let's call the caterer's cooking team and have them cook all the dishes inside campus. People will smell the aroma of the food and this will make this a memorable event." Shravan, the secretary, immediately retorted "Dude, are you sure? Do you think it's practically possible to cook food inside campus for 500 people? It will take at least 5 hours to cook the food." Mekala said, "Exactly. There will be a good build-up to the evening when people see food being cooked, especially Andhra food. It will be a live grill." We had heard of Tandoori grill, but never of Andhra grill. We explored the idea with the caterers. The caterers suggested that it could be possible, but they would need 6 hours to do the cooking.

Mekala convinced the team that we would be trend-setters by following this approach.

The D-day arrived, and along with it, the Great Indian Cooking Circus. 5 tempo travelers came with huge vessels. There were 12 gas cylinders on duty. Mekala was also the team lead for "Project Menu Finalization". He had ensured all the favorite items from Andhra (Gongoora, Pulihora, Mirchi Bhajji, Mammidi Pacchidi, Sambar, Telugu Pappu, Gutha-vankaya kura, Fish curry, etc.) were included in the menu. While this was a lip-smacking menu, it also meant extra hours of cooking and deep-fry. So, the team set up shop from 2 pm and started the process. First, the vegetables were cut. For the first time in my life, I saw 40 kgs of ladies' finger being cut. Tears of joy started rolling when I saw 15 kgs of onion being cut. Parallelly, a separate team was working on the preparations for the rice items. Thankfully, the sweet items were cooked elsewhere and brought in a ready-to-serve form as it would have otherwise taken 2 days to cook them over live counter.

True to Mekala's words, the cooking inside campus generated a lot of curiosity amongst the students. Students would visit the cooking area behind the dinner hall and ask about the dinner start time and the menu. They were all praising team APAXI for their innovative thinking. Mekala was over the moon. Everything was going as per plan. As the rice items were the last to be cooked and served hot, it was decided that the cooking for the rice related items would start by 6:45 pm and finish by 7:30 pm. So, we informed the batch that dinner would be served from 7:30 pm onwards. We wanted to finish the dinner early so we sent an email to all the students with the tagline "Andhra food tastes best when hot. Come early and enjoy hot Andhra meals. Dinner will be closed by 9:30 pm."

At about 7 pm, one of the cooks came to us and said "Sir, there is a problem. The gas stoves are not lighting up. Can you call someone from the college? It's just a small issue and we will be done in 30 minutes once the stoves light up." We asked him "But what if they don't light up?" He said, philosophically, "Bhagwaan aap-ka bhala kare sir[125]." We were getting tensed now. Mekala was nowhere to be seen. We just hoped that the gas problem would go away. Our reputation was now at stake. By trying to be extra innovative when there was no need at all, we looked like making a fool out of ourselves.

By 7:45 pm, people started arriving in hordes. Our tagline "Andhra meals taste best when hot" was proving to be our Achilles heel. We told everyone that there was a slight delay and we would start by 8:30 pm. We had no idea how we would manage in case the stoves didn't light up. We were all nervous like hell. Mekala almost had tears in his eyes.

It was 8:30 pm and the people now had hungry, angry looks on their faces. We could not send them back. As we had announced that the dinner would close by 9:30 pm, almost the whole batch was now at the dinner hall. We became clueless. Prof Reddy was with us overseeing the arrangements. He immediately suggested "Let's not keep the poor students waiting. We will start serving the desserts. I will call my other professor friends to keep rice in their houses and get it cooked. All we need is rice cooked right. If we start now, we will be done by 10 pm. Other things are to be mixed with rice."

We did not like the suggestion but we had no alternate choice. So, we started serving the desserts first. For the first and last time in my life, we only had Jalebi, Mysore-pak, Pootha-

125 May God help you Sir

reykulu and Payasam served without rice items. For a change, we thanked Mekala for the lavish spread he had finalized. Imagine if we only had ordered a single dessert item. People started asking us "Dude, what about the hot Andhra meals and the rice items? Isn't dessert supposed to be in the end?" Our national fruit is banana and national business – "ch*tiya banana[126]". Madhipati told the folks "Guys, in Andhra tradition, desserts are served first. Only then can you appreciate spicy food."

Meanwhile, we asked Prof Reddy to buy us some time by talking and interacting with the students. So, Prof Reddy would go around the hall, chat casually with the students, ask each student how s/he was, which club, etc. We didn't want to do a mass address as this would be done quickly. As a back-up plan, we decided to serve bhajji next and do the cultural performances, this would give time for the rice to come from the other professors' house. We started serving the second round of desserts. One friend asked "Bhai, dessert khilake maar daaloge kya?[127]" The witty Madipathi smilingly replied "Bhai, Andhra dessert ka mazaa kuch aur hi hai. Agar tumne minimum doh baar nahi khaya, toh Andhra food nahi khaya[128]." The crowd was getting impatient now. The first batch was taking too long and the others were getting restless. Some of them started going outside and decided to have food in a restaurant outside campus.

Finally, the first few containers of rice arrived from the Professor's house and we mixed the rice with the pulihora paste and started serving. Again, there was a query "Bhai, only pulihora? What about the other items?"

---

[126] Making a fool out of people

[127] Bro, will you kill us by serving desserts repeatedly?

[128] Unless you eat every dish twice, you haven't had real Andhra food

This time, it was Mekala's turn to hit a sixer. "Bhai, Andhra food is to be tasted sequentially, not parallelly. Isi mey asli mazaa hai[129]." We had no idea how long we could continue this bluff. Prof Reddy came to us and said – "the rice from all of my fellow Prof friends put together will serve one batch of students. After that, we are left with no rice. What do we do?" We quickly convened a meeting of the organizing team. We decided we would call off this bluff, apologize to the batch for trying to be extra-creative and re-organize the dinner. That would be better than giving false hopes to people. The night had gone from bad to worse. We all looked at Mekala and we were kicking ourselves. We decided to make an announcement and walked to the hall. Shravan, the secretary took the mike in his hands "Friends, we have to make an announcement. We are really sorry. . ." Before Shravan could make any announcement, the cook came running and dragged Shravan aside. He said "Sir, finally, the stoves have lit up. Don't ask me how and why. We will be ready in 15 minutes. Please don't call off the dinner." A relieved Shravan continued his announcement "We are really sorry. . . sorry to keep you folks waiting. But in 15 minutes, we will be ready with all the items."

In 20 minutes, hot Andhra meals were finally served to the batch. This time, the desserts were pushed in the end. One of my batchmates asked Madhipati "Dude, for the previous batch, you told desserts would be the starting point as per Andhra tradition. Now, desserts are in the end. What kind of a joke is this?" Before Madhipati could answer, I butted in with a googly, "Dude, there are 3 regions in Andhra Pradesh – Telangana, Rayalseema and coastal Andhra. What the earlier batch saw was the coastal Andhra style, this is now the Rayalseema style."

---

[129] Herein lies the real fun

Thankfully, the folks didn't know much and they were hungry, so they ate whatever was fed.

After that, the rest of the dinner was a breeze. People loved the food and enjoyed the cultural activities. The Yankamma towel dance had the crowd in splits. The others also put up some excellent dance numbers. We thanked Prof Reddy for his support. At the end of the dinner, Venkatesh, the regional secretary of TAXI, the Tamil Nadu association, came to us and said "Well done, folks. Loved the food. The concept of in-house cooking was awesome. Give me the caterer's number. We will try the in-house model for the TAXI dinner as well." A frustrated Sandeep Mekala fittingly replied "Bro, as a well-wisher, never go for in-house catering. Even if you get it at a 50% cheaper rate, I request you to not to go for in-house catering in your life." Venkatesh didn't understand. He came to me and asked "Thambi[130], what's happened to Mekala? Why's he so frustrated?" I replied "Venky, my friend, what you see is not what you get. Let's go for lunch tomorrow to an Andhra mess in Bistupur. I will tell you the whole story. Andhra food tastes best when hot."

130 Brother

11

Last Day Last Date – Kabab mey Haddi[131]

Time went by at the speed of a Shinkansen[132], and before we could realize, we had already completed five trimesters out of six at XL. We wanted to make the most of one last trimester. However, placements were just around the corner. The previous batch had just come out from the Great Recession of 2008-09 and there was a bit of skepticism on whether the entire batch of students would get good job offers. This played in the minds of most of our batchmates and most of them started their placement preparation in the December holiday break of two weeks. Our gang of 8 decided to buck the trend and instead, we went on a trip to Kanha National Park, surrounding Madhya Pradesh. We were clear that destiny would have a key role to play in where we get placed (instead of wasting our holidays by studying). At Kanha, we missed sighting a tiger because I had spent half an hour in the loo and delayed the entire gang. The folks who went in an hour before us told us that they had spotted a tiger. Till today, my friends have not forgiven me for this loo crime. The loo crime reminded me of my childhood astrologer.

---

[131] Mood Spoiler

[132] Japanese bullet train

In my childhood, the first time I had gone to Tirupati, I had met an astrologer. He looked at my palm and told me that I was a habitual loo lover and would spend a minimum of 30 minutes every time I go to the loo. I never met that astrologer after that, but, till date, I remember him for those golden words. His accurate prediction made me a firm believer in astrology, numerology, tarot and all things superstitious. The next year, we wanted to reach out to the same astrologer, but instead, we found another one. This one forecasted that I would have two marriages – one love and the other arranged. The first one would be a love marriage which I would do against my parents' wishes. However, since it would not work out because the girl was from an extremely poor background, I would go on to marry a rich business baron's only daughter. He also predicted that I would be staying with both wives and all three of us would live a troubled life, with each trying to manage the other two. My mother was around when she heard this prediction and started laughing. I took this prediction a bit too seriously and decided I will not have a girlfriend. Why put someone through the misery? The astrologer also told me not to wear anything black. My mother, this time though, was serious and told me never to wear black. Hence, "black" and "girlfriend" were erased from my dictionary.

I knew for sure that it was always going to be an arranged marriage, given my family's fetish for all things superstitious. I also heard a few horror stories from my friends about how having a girlfriend took a toll on their academics. *Saalon ko Malai bhi chahiye aur makkhan bhi*[133]. I used to admire the cool dudes on campus who would do well in the academic world as well as the offline world. Some would go a step further and

[133] The buggers wanted to have the cake and eat it, too

have two girlfriends simultaneously. The coolness quotient in campus would be determined by the hotness of the girlfriend one would have. I was least fazed by all of this. I was sure that I would not have one as I was scared that getting into a relationship would have its academic side effects. Whenever I would think of having one, the image of the astrologer with the Bermuda triangle would appear in front of me. So, I decided to be happily single and ever ready to mingle.

In those days, having a girlfriend was an expensive affair, especially if you had still not found a job. You needed to take her to fancy restaurants, buy clothes for her birthdays, etc. However, I also wanted to ensure that I was not a nerdy geek who could not strike a conversation with a girl, as I would face problems later in my arranged marriage girl-hunt. Therefore, I adopted a "committed dates" strategy. I used to ask out committed girls in campus, who were friends with me, for dinner/lunch dates. For them, it was just a casual dine-out and for me it was just a friendly chat. This also used to make some of the boys jealous. They were shocked to see how a seedha-saadha[134] nerdy like me could go out for dinner dates with some of the hottest committed girls on campus.

My last date on campus was with Apurva. Apurva was a pretty and hard-working girl. She was a member of Sigma (the social initiatives club at XL) and had a huge fan-following amongst the boys. I asked her out for lunch. She gracefully obliged and said she would meet me for lunch on the last day of campus and from there on, head towards the railway station to meet her boyfriend in Kolkata. We decided to go to Novelty Restaurant in Bistupur. It was an Italian fine-dining restaurant. Apurva and I left from campus in an auto-rickshaw. As our

---

[134] Naive

auto passed through the exit gates, I could already hear a few of the boys gasping with their mouth wide open, looking at the two of us heading out. I got a text from one of my friends "Lord saale, bada khiladi nikla bey tu to[135]". I decided to keep my phone in silent mode for the next few hours. Already, I had ruffled a few feathers. I just wanted to have a good time with Apurva.

We entered Novelty restaurant and ordered starters. Novelty was opposite another restaurant called Sonnet. Sonnet had a buffet lunch for about 500 bucks and usually, most of the XL folks would be found there. Novelty was a quieter place during the afternoons. While we were getting down from the auto, I saw a bunch of my classmates coming out from Sonnet. Poojitha, Siddharth (the Arjuna awardee in our summer internship), Mohsin, Prashanth and a few others were smiling at us. We smiled back and went in. We ordered starters – Veg Manchurian and cheese balls. We were chatting away for a while. Suddenly, Apurva gestured me to look behind. She was smiling. I turned around and to my surprise, I saw Bhai (my classmate who had spoken about J & J in the Pepsi interview) sitting alone. He ordered fresh lime soda. We thought that he was waiting for someone. Maybe, he too had come out on a date. We waved at him. He waved back. Apurva and I continued chatting. But then Apurva told me Bhai was constantly looking at us and maybe we should invite him to our table just for a few minutes if I was ok. I was fine, just a few minutes and Bhai would then go his way. We called Bhai to our table. We chatted casually for a few minutes, until it started to get annoying. We thought Bhai would leave but he

---

135 Lord you bugger!! You turned out to be quite a player

was stuck to the chair like a Fevicol[136] box. Apurva messaged me saying "Hari, I think you should ask him to politely leave" The starters came, bhai said he was not hungry and he was almost done. But Bhai gobbled up half the starters, he also munched off a few pizza slices. Ironically, both Apurva and I were vegetarians and we did not order a chicken bone. Else, we would have symbolically ordered chicken seekh kebab along with a *haddi*[137] as a tribute to Bhai. The worst part was, whenever I tried to strike a conversation with Apurva on a random topic, Bhai would butt in and give his unsolicited opinion. His lustful eyes did more talking than his words. For about 45 minutes, Bhai's torture continued. Apurva was now visibly getting fidgety. She said her train would depart in some time and she should leave now. My last date was crushed with ill fate. Bhai asked us "You guys don't want to have desserts?" I wanted to kick him so hard that he would land in the Thar desert. Imagine this. Which sane person in this world, would randomly come in, spoil a date by sticking around and still have the audacity to have a dessert. Apurva ended the torture by saying "Mr. ****** (Bhai's real name), I think I really have to leave." I offered to drop her to the station. Bhai, the great despo of Ball Street, butted in again "Even I will join you guys, if you don't mind."

We were shocked. How could anyone be so shameless and still boldly talk like this? I wanted to kill Bhai then and there but before I could do anything, Apurva interjected "Bhai, I think you are not getting it. This was supposed to be a date where two people would just have a casual conversation and have a good time. This is not funny anymore. I think you should

136 Glue

137 Bone

respect people's privacy." I guess Bhai had decided that he was Sallu Bhai. *Bhai ko kya farak padtha? Duniya bhai key peeche hai - Bhai duniye key peeche nahi.* [138] He smiled and said "Chill man, as it was casual, I thought there was place for me." I guess he had taken the word casual, a bit too casually, or maybe a bit too seriously. Like a *bahu*[139] who is reluctant on her *bidaai*[140], Bhai bid farewell to us and left. He had gracefully ruined my last date at XL and ensured that I would never forget this date.

Apurva, meanwhile, seemed to have read my mind. We laughed along on the way in the auto-rickshaw and I dropped her at the station. I hoped that the train would arrive late and I could get some more time. But *hamaari ghatiya kismat*[141] would continue that day. The train's starting point was Jameshedpur, and any such hopes were promptly dashed when the announcer screamed *"Mitron, Steel Express agle 5 minutes mey nikalne waali hai... Aur meri zindagi bhi jhand hone waali hai... Aur hari ki humesha gaa^du kismat hi hai... Dhanyavaad Dhanyavaad*[142]*"*

The train left and Apurva waved goodbye. When I was back in campus, my last date had become the talk of the college. People who did not know about Bhai's presence, came and asked "Dude, how was your date? You are rocking, man. Going out for dates with Apurva!! Lucky you." When I told them about Bhai's antics, they couldn't stop laughing. Some wanted to do a social boycott of Bhai. Himanshu Joshi wanted to have some fun

---

[138] What difference does it make to Bhai? The world runs behind Bhai and not the other way around

[139] Daughter-in-law

[140] When daughter moves away from parents to be with in-laws

[141] My bad luck

[142] Friends! The Steel Express is going to depart in 5 minutes. And Hari is always going to have rotten luck

and decided to start "Bhai ki aadalat[143]", where Bhai would be grilled. But I knew Bhai would not take it sportingly. I told them to let it go. I would have my revenge on Bhai sometime later. I had a one-on-one with Bhai but he apologized and said it was just by chance he was having lunch in the same place and he did not mean it. I thought it was true. But later, Poojitha (whom I had seen walking out of Sonnet that day) told me the real story. She said Bhai had seen us going in while he was with them and he had already finished his lunch. But seeing me going in with Apurva, he decided to show who was the real Bhai.

After listening to this, I made an on-the-spot dating rulebook, which I always carry with me, in my mind and heart:

Rule #1: Never agree for a date on the day someone has a train/ flight/bus.

Rule #2: Never select a place which is commonly frequented, or which is close to a commonly frequented place.

Rule #3: Always ignore anyone you bump into and change your restaurant if you find any such people.

The most important rule:

Rule #4: Bhai log sey door rehna[144]. Dekhte Dekhte g**nd maarke nikal jayenge.

---

143 Court testimony of Bhai

144 Stay away from Bhais. They will screw you without even you realizing.

12

XL Meri Jaan[145]

Our last term at XL was a mixed bag. While we were happy to have gotten placed in companies with an attractive salary (Some folks do not agree because no CTC is good enough for them) and get into the next phase of life, we were all sad that we would miss the best phase of our lives. Each of us had their own memories of the hallowed portals. Some found their love, some their dream jobs, some a great set of friends, some had their trips and treks, some achieved sporting glory, some, like me, just went with the flow.

Apart from the highs, XL also gave us a set of lows. The XL-IIM C annual sports meet was one example. While we were juniors, we hosted the meet and lost it by 0. 33 points (9. 66 -9. 33). One of our seniors had missed the sudden-death penalty, and for this, he became the Kabir Khan (SRK in Chak De India who gets vilified for missing the penalty in the movie's opening sequence) of our campus. The next year, when were seniors, we thought we will wrest the trophy at Joka (Calcutta), but we got thrashed 21-2. XL-IIMC was like India-Pakistan, and we had lost tamely. This was an unforgettable low point.

There were some unforgettable happy memories as well. XL in those days was famous for "Wet Nights". My wife, who

[145] My Life

is a doctor, finds this name extremely nauseating, but Wet Nights used to happen after Dry Days. There would be a batch party with a DJ and people would dance away to glory till early morning. Wet Nights were a microcosm of our society. A significant majority of the students would love the wet nights as it would give them a chance to unwind. There was a Leftist population which would boycott this due to various reasons, like sound pollution, conscience pollution, dance pollution, couple's pollution, etc. Most teetotalers barring me would stay away from the Wet Nights. I used to love them for three reasons –

#1 I could dance to my heart's content

#2 The Graveyard DJ shift by my friend Shivam Naman Sinha

#3 The post 3 am tamasha[146].

After a few pegs down, it was funny to see couples changing hands, random people dancing with each other, crying, etc. On our last Wet Night (the day of our convocation), a few of us cried a lot… Let me digress for a minute. XLRI Jamshedpur was the best thing to have happened to me in my professional career. Before XL, I was a nobody. In our society, which emphasizes more on brands and name tags and less on the product, XLRI made me feel I was a somebody. As soon as I received my XL admit card, I felt that I had arrived in this world, finally. In India, if you say you are an IIT-ian, many people suddenly start pouring liters of milk over you (the preparation for IIT starts as early as class 6 in some cases). If you are a random somebody from a random unbranded school, college, the ISHMBC (Indian society of mediocrity, hypocrisy and brand consciousness) ensures you continue to live a random life. Once

[146] Performance

I graduated from XLRI, I felt nothing is impossible. I got the quiet confidence to take on the world. Coming from a humble middle-class family where the highest educated persons were graduates, XLRI gave me wings. A picture is worth a thousand words and a million words. The pride in my parents' eyes when they saw my convocation photo of my XLRI degree being given by Mr. Muthuraman (then MD of Tata Steel and Chairman of the XLRI Board) said it all. I had arrived in this world. At that time, I had decided that if at all I write my first book, then a complete chapter will be dedicated to XL.

Coming back to the last Wet Night on campus, many of us cried a lot after it got over. In the wee hours of the morning while I was walking back to my room one last time, I decided to let out my emotions via a written note. As I try to pursue an alternate career as a writer, it is only fitting that I reproduce my first article – XL Meri Jaan, which was written as a Facebook note on that morning, post our last Wet Night (a tribute to my alma mater XL).

If you are an XLer, you will cry reading this piece. If you are not an XLer but you still have good memories of your college, your heart will skip a beat. Here you go.

"XL Meri Jaan"

It's my first note on FB, and probably my last, too. I honestly don't know why I am writing this. All along this 2-year journey, my aim was to get out with a decent job and I thought that was all that mattered to me. As a result, I must confess that I really did not feel a sense of attachment to this place, for most part. I always used to wonder why many of my batchmates, seniors, used to get emotional every time "XL meri jaan" was played. But today, as the song was played one last time at our last wet night, I suddenly felt a sense of emptiness. There was this eerie feeling that something was being taken away from me, and trust me, I am not being melodramatic here. It dawned on me that in a few days from now, all of this is going to come to an end. People around are going to go their own ways, carve their future, in the dog-eat-dog corporate world. Those who have worked prior in organizations will probably empathize with me. Despite all the grumblings people may have had with respect to submissions, quizzes, grades, mess food, GBMs[147], politics, cramped academic schedule etc., one thing is for sure, this two-year life will be missed sorely. Ratanjee, XL-IIMC, Bishuda, Dadu, Regional committee dinners and so on… … … …. People might treasure different memories, for different reasons. But let's face it, I don't think we will ever get to be awake at 3 am, have a fried Maggi, or go for a walk. This is just an example of those innumerable moments, which might look small at this point, but will surely be missed. The 2-year honeymoon is over, and it's time to pass the baton as one more batch moves out of XL.

Now, for the first time, after the Candles which our seniors had lit up before Punch Nite, I feel a sense of attachment to this place. I now understand why all those souls got emotional each time "XL meri jaan" was played. Its 6:30 am as I am writing this, probably one of those last few times when I am awake the whole night without any care as to what's going to happen next. I don't know how to end this post, so will end it with those very lines,

Karke Humey Bekaraar… Meri Jaan… …O Meri Jaan…

XL.... thanks for all the memories

[147] General Body Meetings

13

Idli. com

After a fun filled two years at XL, it was time to set foot into the corporate world. We were asked to report to the Mumbai head office of WIMC. The first day was quite eventful. I had been warned against taking the local train. But me being me, I had the itch of venturing into the unknown, especially when people advised against something. I boarded the train at Ghatkopar. Everything was normal until the train stopped at Kurla, the next station. Here, a sea of people entered the train. Like waves in a beach, which push you a few inches back, I was automatically pushed from the wash basin area to the toilet. No big deal – I thought to myself. It was pretty much a normal journey so far. After Kurla, the people getting into the train started increasing disproportionately. The train resembled an over-inflated balloon which could burst any moment. A few people were hanging near the door. However, it seemed though I was more worried about their lives than the folks themselves. These folks seemed to relish the breeze coming in from the outside. For the rest of us, it was a cauldron of sweat. My private parts started to itch with sweat but I had no place to even put my hand down and scratch, as I was sandwiched between eight people. This was worse than a concentration camp. For a moment, I feared that maybe an insect had entered my pants and was responsible for the itch. The scary thought of dying a virgin entered my head. Before I could think further, Dadar station arrived.

My stop was Elphinston Road, which was two stations away, but because I was standing in the direction of the exit, I was promptly thrown out of the train at Dadar. Behind me, a million folks got down from the train. It was as if they had been liberated from a jail after serving 15 plus years of rigorous imprisonment. I somehow got back into the train. It wasn't me who was responsible for this. Because I stared in the direction of the entrance from the outside, I was pushed inside by a tsunami-like unstoppable force of people. Mashallah![148] What an experience. I wanted to get out of this hell-hole asap but it took me another ten minutes to do so. Those ten minutes were pure torture. I was drowned in an ocean of sweat. It looked like my white ironed shirt had cried as if it was beaten to death. It was a sea of water, rather salted sweat. My first day was doomed.

Inspired by James Bond, I had chosen a white Arrow shirt and a black trouser for my first day. By the time I got out, the white shirt had become grey. My black trouser absorbed all the external heat and ensured that I would never wear a black trouser in Mumbai again. As I got out at Elphinston Road, I felt relieved. I thought I had escaped slavery from the Britishers. I could see the relief amongst my fellow passengers who had gotten down. One nice soul seemed to have read my mind and told me, "Dude, I always get an extra pair of clothes – one for the train and one for the office." What an insight. Before I could think further, I noticed something amiss. Everything around me was crystal clear and white. I thought somebody had flicked my spectacles in the train. But no. The spectacles were intact. The

[148] Goodness

only difference was there were no lens. I ran my fingers through the spectacles. The glass lens were victims of the train. That was it. I vowed never to take a train to the office again. On the way, I bought another shirt and reported at the Headquarters.

I narrated this incident to the folks at office. They were not surprised and advised to take a taxi to office instead. It sounded like a great idea. So that same evening, at around 6:30 pm, I decided to take a taxi from Worli to Ghatkopar. My friend Vaibhav, who had also joined the same organization, had to go to Delhi the same evening. We both left the office at the same time. It took almost 3. 5 hours for me to go from Worli to Ghatkopar, thanks to the traffic. As I was about to reach home at about 10 pm, I got a call from Vaibhav. He said he had reached home in Delhi. The time taken to go from Mumbai to Delhi was lesser than Worli to Ghatkopar. What an eventful first day. The only silver lining was that I did not have to waste another shirt in the cab.

After an eventful train and cab journey on my first day, the next few days were routine in nature, without much action. I was placed in the Group HR team handling the B-school management trainee program related activities on campus. Part of the job entailed travelling to India's top B-schools. My first corporate travel was slotted for the coming Monday. Me and my colleague Salim were supposed to take a 7 am flight to Lucknow. We had to go to IIM Lucknow for a campus engagement. In those days, Kingfisher airlines was the default choice for corporate travel, thanks to the beautiful air-hostesses. Being my first flight in my corporate career, I arrived 45 minutes prior to check-in. The boarding gates would close at 6:30 am. Having arrived at 5:45 am, I decided to complete my security check and wait for Salim. Salim arrived at 6:00 am and we finished the security check in 5 minutes. With 25 minutes still left, we decided to have an idli at a shop named idli. com, located in the centre of the airport food-court. Being a South Indian, idli was my favorite dish and I couldn't resist the temptation of having an early morning idli breakfast. We finished our idlis in 10 minutes. 15 minutes were still left for the gates to close. Salim prodded me to go to the boarding gates but I remembered a golden advice from one of my friends. He had told me - "Once you have collected your boarding pass, there is no way on earth you can miss a flight, as the airline will announce your name and only after the passenger boards, will the flight take off." I gave this gyaan to Salim and we continued to chat at idli. com.

It was 6:30 a. m. and there was no announcement. One of the flight attendants came to the food court area and shouted- "Final boarding call for Kingfisher Airlines Lucknow !!!" Salim wanted to leave but I confidently told him, "Dude, let's wait for the announcement. What a proud moment it will be when the airline will announce our names. And then we will be the last people to board the flight, like kings. Since we have our boarding passes, no one can do anything to us." 5 more minutes passed and the announcement didn't arrive yet.

Suddenly, a chill ran through my spine. What if we could not make it? Only 25 minutes were left. We decided we would not take any chances now. We ran as fast as we could to the boarding gates. We confidently showed our boarding passes to the attendants. They just smiled and said "Sorry, sir. The gates are closed." We tried our best to convince, request and finally cried and begged them to let us in. We told them that our jobs were on the line if we missed this flight. None of the emotional angles worked. Our luggage was brought back and handed over to us.

We were screwed. Despite arriving 30 minutes prior, I had overconfidently assumed no one could do anything. I wanted to kill my friend who had given me the boarding pass logic. More importantly, we feared our boss. No explanation would be of use in such a scenario. The organization would ask us to foot our own tickets. We had to go to Lucknow that day. The next available flight's ticket cost was around 10,000 rupees. We almost wanted to cry.

Salim was the calmer of the two. Between the two of us, we decided that it would be him, who would speak to our boss about the incident. He spoke to our boss for 15 minutes and came away smiling. He said the company would book us on the next available reasonably priced flight. I was amazed by Salim. I felt proud of Salim for having told the truth. The respect for my boss increased because he had accepted our mistake and yet booked us on the next flight.

As we got our tickets in our mailbox, I congratulated Salim. I appreciated him for his honesty. He retorted - "Dude, there's no honesty business. Had we been honest, our jobs would have been on the line. I told boss that our laptops were exchanged during the security check with another gentleman. By the time there was an announcement regarding this and the gentleman returned the laptops, the boarding gates had closed and we were not allowed entry for no fault of ours. Now you also stick to this story, else we will be fired."

It was less than 10 days in this organization, and because of an idli and a boarding pass, I had almost messed it up. Till this day, whenever I eat an idli, I can't help but think of idli. com and the missed Kingfisher flight. I always go straight to the boarding gates, and have stopped having breakfast at the airport.

14

Rocket Singh in Las Vegas

After the idli.com fiasco, I was much sharper and wiser, while travelling on the job. I lived out of a suitcase for the first two years of my corporate career. I travelled the length and breadth of the country to recruit students from the top B schools of the country. The role helped improve my personality by leaps and bounds as I was giving a corporate presentation to B school students almost every third day, interviewing students, negotiating placement slots, shortlisting resumes, working on strengthening the employer brand and doing a host of other related activities. During the course of my campus travels, I also had the opportunity to network with senior HR and business leaders. The more I spoke to various people, the more I became convinced that I was not cut out for HR. When my career planning discussion came up after two years, I informed my reporting manager that I wanted to move out of HR. He was a gem at heart, so he advised me to start off my business career with Sales. One thing led to another and within a span of 3 months, I was posted as an Area Sales Manager (ASM) managing the districts of Nashik and Jalgaon.

I think I was the first person in WIMC, as well as my XLRI class, to move from HR to Sales. The house was divided on the probability of my success. A few colleagues questioned the use of my HR degree from the best HR institute in Asia, while some praised me for a brave move. A few of them laughed at me initially saying that I had made the biggest mistake of my life by leaving a cushy HR job and going for the slog. For the first three months, I was not sure if I had made the right decision. I was working hard and slogging it out, but the expectations from me were sky-high. I was expected to do better than the regular ASMs as I was from a premium B school. The pressure was getting to me. Not the pressure of sales numbers, but the weight of managing the lofty expectations.

Unsure of my next move, I went to my HR mentor and told him to help me get back in an HR role at the earliest. My confidence was at an all-time low. But mentors are mentors for a reason. My mentor was one of the senior-most HR leaders in the organization. He told me that he was backing me, come what may, and I should not take such a hasty decision without experiencing the full 12-month sales cycle. If required, he would have a word with my Zonal Sales Manager to ensure that I succeed. When you have such senior people backing you in the not-so-good times, it makes a world of difference to your confidence. I don't know how my mentor had seen potential in me and what made him back me. All I know is after that conversation, I went back stronger and decided that at any cost, I am not going to let him down and not give up. That 45-minute conversation removed all the negativities that I had and I decided to focus only on what I could control, the inputs.

In October 2013, the organization launched a sales contest – "Gaadi Becho, Duniya Dekho[149]". The rules of the game were very simple. The top 30 ASMs from a pool of 200 pan India would win a trip to either of the three destinations – Las Vegas, Rome or Singapore. The targets were very steep and all of us felt

[149] Sell Vehicles, Travel the World as a reward

that they were highly unrealistic. We were asked to do 3 times our current monthly average. Most folks wanted to give up. One man, though, had other ideas. It was our Zonal Head (ZH). He was clear in his mind that West Zone would sell 25,000 vehicles and most of us from West would qualify for the trip. He crafted a theme "Mission 25000" and termed his army as "Western Warriors".

There was a 2 day kick off session in Garudmachi, a hill-station close to Pune. A motivational speaker was called and by the end of two days, all of us in the West Zone truly believed that we would sell 25,000 vehicles. The same figures for the same period in the previous year were 16,000. Our ZH ensured that the momentum of Western Warriors did not fizzle out after the kick-off event. Success stories were shared, an email chain was created with dashboards, updates, small celebrations and con-calls were held every few days.

As an ASM, we had to spend a minimum of 21 days every month in our markets, but those three months, the entire West Zone team was out in the market on all working days. I travelled the length and breadth of Nashik and Jalgaon, going to tehsils like Dindori, Niphad, Amalner, and Raver (names which I had never heard of). I used to go with the team and try and close bookings. The joy of converting a sale was unparalleled. Because of a senior person visiting, a lot of customers' purchase decision would be fast-tracked. The sales team at the dealerships also started believing that the targets could be achieved. If the inputs are right, the output will also fall in place. By the end of December, Western Warriors had sold a whopping 27,000 vehicles. West Zone had the highest ASMs qualifying for Las Vegas. Thanks to a fantastic show by both my dealerships (Nashik won the best debutant award and Jalgaon won the best upcountry performance in our Area Office), yours truly also qualified for Las Vegas, along with 4 other colleagues from Mumbai Area Office. I had never imagined in the wildest of my dreams, that I would move to Sales.

From being someone who almost wanted to quit sales to being amongst the country's top 30, it was quite a turn-around for me. There was a new-found confidence in me that Sales was "the" place to be. High pressure, but completely worth it. In Sales, a person is as good as his last month's performance, just like a cricketer. If you are out of form, you are out of the scheme of things. But there-in lies the fun. The ones who figure out the basics continue to have sustained success. The flashes in the pan fizzle out. Thankfully, I had slogged continuously in my first twelve months in sales and it made me extremely grounded and extremely strong in my basics. From then on, there was no looking back, and the next 6 years of my career, I rocked in the sales function. At least I thought so.

Las Vegas was literally a dream come true. We spent 2 nights in Los Angeles and 4 nights in Vegas. I was amazed to see a 25 square km strip of land being transformed into one of the world's most expensive places to live in. We spent every night partying, sat in a limousine, gambled in a few of the world's richest casinos, and did some shopping in Fremont Street. Contrary to its perception as a "Sin city", Vegas had a huge number of families visiting along with kids. Vegas had something for everyone. There were replicas of Disneyland, the Taj Mahal and the Eiffel Tower. There were some astounding adventure rides at the top of sky-scrapers. The city, or rather, the Strip, was also home to a lot of theatre performances. Vegas also has a famous church, where you can get married and divorced in two minutes, legally. It wasn't only about sex and strip clubs, contrary to the popular perception.

Our experience with strip clubs, though, was surreal. One day, we decided that we would visit all the famous clubs and paint the town red. We were four of us. We called up a strip club and asked for a pick-up at sharp 9 pm. The driver arrived at sharp 9 pm at our hotel. It was a typical Indian group of friends, and 9 pm by Indian standards meant a delay of minimum 20 minutes. The driver patiently waited till we arrived. Once all of us arrived, he gave us a mouthful. "Folks, you are not in India. You are in Vegas. Time is money here and money is time. F**k you guys. I waited to give you a piece of my mind and remind you that you are in Vegas. I am leaving now. You can find an alternate transport. I have already informed the club to blacklist you folks and you will never be offered any pick-ups." He left us stranded. We never thought a cab driver would put us in our place in Vegas.

Having learnt our lesson, we took a cab outside the hotel and went to the first club. The atmosphere was electric. We were offered a grand welcome and we witnessed a sensuous pole dance. We wanted to go to the front but we were warned by a fellow Indian that going in the front means throwing a few dollars for every person walking on the stage. The four of us made our mental calculations that money spent splurging on drinks is better than money spent on a dancer. So, we had a few drinks (being a teetotaler, I had a Red bull) sitting in the back rows. Quite a few ladies approached us for a lap dance. We were initially tempted but one of our friends told us that the next strip club had the best lap dance experiences and we should try it there. Enlightened by his knowledge, we decided to proceed to the next strip club.

This was one of the most famous clubs in Vegas and was a huge hit amongst the locals. After a happy experience with the first club, we wanted to show off and decided that we would not visit any further clubs but spend all our money in this one club and spend the night here. Based on our previous learning, we decided to head straight to the front row near the stage with all our remaining savings. A bouncer stopped us. We were asked to shell 10 dollars per person for sitting in the front row. It was no small amount but one of our friends told us that 10 dollars is no big amount for spending a full night in front of the stage at the best strip club in Vegas. He was right. The four of us put together gave 40 dollars. We had 60 left but we didn't care. As soon as we sat in the front seat, the first pole dancer came and showed off her moves. It was time to tip. We threw 10 dollars but the dancer gave an angry scowl. She whispered something in the bouncer's ear. The bouncer was walking furiously towards us. Before he could come closer, one of our friends threw another 10-dollar note at the dancer. She signaled something to the bouncer, and he stopped. This was not the Vegas experience we had hoped for. We barely relaxed for a couple of minutes when a waitress approached us asking for a drinks order. We gave 20 dollars with each drink costing 5 dollars. To our surprise, she came back with only 3 drinks. She had taken 5 dollars as a tip. We were now left with only 20 dollars. My optimist friend told us that we will not order any drink for the next few hours. After all, we had entered the front row, paid our tips when requested. By the time we could think any further, the next pole dancer arrived. Another 20 dollars went down the drain, or rather, the pole. We were now out of money. We didn't know what to do. We decided to put a brave face. Immediately, the waitress came again for the next order. We protested. The waitress signaled to the bouncer. Before he could make his move, we made ours. We quietly exited the place.

As we had boastfully told our office colleagues that we were heading to the most happening strip club in Vegas, the next day over breakfast, a few colleagues were asking us for recommendations for strip clubs to visit. Before we could reply, our optimist friend who had suggested the strip club idea replied on our behalf - "Folks, we all are in Vegas. Here, time is money and money is time. Everyone in this city is aligned to this philosophy. You will understand when you visit the club."

It is no wonder that people say "What happens in Vegas... stays in Vegas!!"

15

Arranged-Marriage.Com

The Las Vegas trip was an unforgettable one. It was even more special as it was my first ever international trip. After this achievement, my self-confidence in sales soared sky-high and there was no looking back. Thanks to my stellar performance as an Area Sales Manager, I was interviewed for the role of an Executive Assistant (E. A) to the National Sales Head in 2014. I cleared the interview and moved on to the Head Office in Mumbai. I was 27 years old by then, and being the only child, it was already getting late for marriage by traditional South Indian standards. I had postponed this subject discussion for the past two years but I had to now find a girl through the "arranged" route. Having an MBA degree from one of India's most reputed B schools and working in Mumbai, I thought that it would be a cakewalk for me. But it wasn't to be. The search process took close to 3 years. By the end of it, I was so frustrated that I wanted to pen down a memoir about my quest to find a girl.

It all started with a newspaper matrimonial ad. I was initially resistant to place an ad for myself in the newspaper as I thought it was equivalent to putting myself up for sale. But my parents and well-wishers told me that for an arranged marriage, an "omni-channel marketing strategy" was required. Newspaper ads, online matrimonial sites, offline marriage meets, temples, astrologers, friends' circle and priests. These were the various channels which were recommended. The only thing left was me beating myself on the chest with a board hanging over my neck with the words "Hey folks, I desperately want to get married. Please help me." Other than this, all possible sources and channels were used.

The newspapers had a standard template for the matrimonial ads. Only name and email id were allowed to be changed. I had no option but to go with their rules and regulations. "A 6ft tall, fair and handsome, Mumbai based Brahmin Iyer boy is looking for a slim, fair, tall and beautiful working girl (Iyers preferred). Contact XXX."

If you ever read the Sunday matrimonial section of any newspaper, you will find hordes of tall, fair, handsome and horny Indian bridegrooms up for sale. All these males would be looking for the following combination – slim, tall, fair and beautiful girls. I used to wonder if India even had these many girls who were having all of those four characteristics in unison.

After the newspaper ad, came the website. My parents were not very tech-savvy, so I created my profile and operated it with my dad's login (in those days, a groom directly contacting the girl's parents to initiate an alliance was unacceptable). I created a new Gmail account on behalf of my father and used to write to prospective fathers-in-law with a standard template - "Dear Sir/ Ma'am, we are interested in your daughter's profile. In case you are interested, please share your contact number". A lot of times, I would get calls from the prospective bride's parents "Sir, we want our daughter to speak to your son" I would change my voice to sound like my dad and ask them to call at my alternate number. Initially, I had uploaded a few "candid" photos on my matrimonial profile, but again, my well-wishers told me to upload only a few selected photo-shopped pics.

It did not end there. As I had taken a "premium" membership, I was assigned a "relationship" manager who recommended that I get a proper marriage photo-shoot done. As she was the "subject matter expert", I got a photo-shoot done. I was made to pose with a fake "This is the happiest moment in my life" smile by the photographer. It took about 10 re-takes to get "the" photo right as I couldn't fake the smile properly initially. As per the photographer, sometimes I was a bit too serious, sometimes I blushed a lot. At the 9th re-take, I threatened to walk out and finally, the photographer clicked me as he was left with no other choice. He again remarked that my smile seemed sheepish and if given a couple of more retakes, he could get me "the" pose. I was in no mood to take any of this any further and walked out with the photograph in hand.

The relationship manager then advised me to post a few "cool" hobbies, like photography, painting, playing music, etc. in my profile. I told her that I was no way creative in all this. She said that this was the way to make my profile "stand-out" from the crowd. Reluctantly, I put up "basketball" as my hobby as I had played basketball once in engineering, so it was good enough to qualify as a hobby. I also put up "table tennis", although I hadn't played it since school. This matrimony profile-building reminded me of my "CV building" days for the MBA summer internship. I decided to block the "relationship" manager after this.

After the profile building stage, the dreaded "horoscope" matching process arrived. Initially, my parents were particularly fussy about the horoscopes being matched. As we didn't have a family astrologer, we decided to approach a "freelancer". We came to know about this astrologer in a temple. This freelancer used to operate out of a school in Chembur[150]. Every alternate Sunday, I would download about 20 profiles and go to this man along with my parents. He would categorize the horoscopes into three categories "Excellent match", "average match" and "outright rejects". The best part about these "excellent matches" was that they used to get outrightly rejected by the opposite party's astrologer. The average matches would be "passed through" but my parents were scared that an average match would result in an average marriage, so we did not go ahead. A lot of times, the opposite party would call us saying the horoscope match was "excellent", only for our freelancer to label it "outright" reject. Days passed by and we couldn't find an "excellent match" from both sides. My parents were getting worried now.

Already, a year had passed. We decided to try another freelancer, but the same story repeated. Then, one fine day, we did the unthinkable. We went to the Chembur temple and prayed to God to forgive us. Forgive us because we decided to abandon the horoscope and move ahead. We changed the status in our matrimonial website profile to "horoscope not mandatory" and proceeded further. It was a big relief as we had eliminated a big road-block.

After doing away with the horoscope, we proceeded to the next phase. With each passing day, it felt as if finding a girl through the arranged marriage route was the equivalent of clearing the final round of Kaun Banega Crorepati[151]. After every few days, there seemed to be eliminations on certain

---

150 A suburb in Mumbai

151 India's version of Who Wants to Be a Millionaire

"incorrect" answers in the telephonic discussions. Most families were obsessed with the groom "owning" a house. In most cases, people would ignore my educational qualification and drop the alliance when they figured out that we didn't have an "own" house. The logic was that the groom would not provide for a "stable life" as the family didn't have a house of their own. For somebody who had just started working, owning a house in Mumbai was the equivalent of the Indian football team qualifying for the World Cup in four years' time from now. Theoretically possible but practically impossible. Somehow, the bride's side would never understand this. Having learnt our lesson that the "own house" was a stumbling block despite my academic credentials, we used to start our discussions with an upfront statement that "We don't have an own house. Is it ok with you?" To a lot of people, it sounded rude, but that was the only way ahead. Many so called "modern liberal" families were still deep-rooted in their love for an "own" house.

For those families who were okay with "no horoscope match" and "no own house", there came a "teesra padaav[152]"- the "Mumbai" factor. The parents of Mumbai based brides wanted me to settle in Mumbai forever. For those not from Mumbai, they felt it was an expensive city and they were looking for grooms settled in Bangalore, Hyderabad or Chennai. Either way, we got jacked. I never knew that an arranged marriage would have so many decision-making factors. I did not have a definite answer to either of the two questions.

Then came the next barrier – the overseas obsession. "We want our girl to settle abroad. Will the groom shift abroad in the next two years? We are receiving lot of offers from IT professionals who are already "on-site" and are ready to get green

[152] The third filter

cards." By then, the only card I had was my Aadhaar[153] card. The organization I was working with was an India-headquartered MNC. People had gone on international postings, but this was not my aspiration. Another set of prospects got wiped out.

Two years had passed already in this stage and I was yet to actually meet a girl in person. In most cases, even if the above filters were cleared, I would get clean bowled at the telephonic discussions. As it was telephonic, I used to keep discussions with girls very crisp and would reserve deeper conversations for face-to-face meeting. But I guess most girls found this "un-interesting" and hence the next round would never happen. One girl was working for an automobile client in a reputed IT organization. Because I was also working in an automobile company, I had asked a few questions regarding her nature of work, her travel schedules, etc. The girl found me a bit too "nosy" for an initial discussion and I got slammed again.

In between all this, my parents were getting highly tensed. Tensed more because of the societal pressures. Our relatives and well-wishers added fuel to the fire with their unwanted sympathies "Oh, two years and your boy hasn't found a match yet. Must be a horoscope issue. We will do some pujas on your behalf." Our society's favorite pastime is to pass unnecessary comments on others when not asked. We went to Varanasi, Madurai and Shirdi to pray and hope that this arranged marriage ordeal would end quickly.

I guess the Gods smiled on us, because, after these visits, some face-to-face discussions started happening. This was also due to the fact that my parents had removed all the initial "criteria". The Iyer girl criterion went out of the window. So did

[153] National Personal Identification

the "vegetarian" and the "horoscope" criteria. In fact, they got so frustrated that they asked me to "find" a girl in office. They used to talk to my friends and ask them for references. Purely to see a smile on my parents' face, I had decided that I would say "yes" to the first girl I met face-to-face. I had assumed that my XLRI degree and a decent personality would make the opposite side fall for me. I had under-estimated the opinion of the brides' parents.

I went to Bangalore with my parents to meet my first alliance. The girl and me liked each other. But the girl's father was a retired military man. He said he would send his relatives to my office as well as my house to meet me. We called this off as we did not want such a controlling personality. We then went to Jaipur. Again, both liked each other. After this was expressed, I told the girl's parents about an earlier illness which my mom had which was now under control. But the girl's parents freaked out. We even made them speak to our family doctor, but to no avail. My parents felt bad for me. After that, I decided I would not open this topic again with the fear of getting rejected.

We then met another family in Chembur. Again, both of us liked each other but the girl told me her father didn't like me and she couldn't go against her father. I wondered who I was getting married to – the girl or her father? I tried to convince the girl but I guess it was too late. Then onwards, I would not let my parents travel with me, especially for outstation flight visits, as it was an expensive affair without results. I decided that I would do the initial round and if things progressed, my parents would go in. I travelled to Ahmedabad, Kolkata, and a few other locations, and completed a Bharat Darshan[154] in my quest to find a girl. A couple of times, I rejected the opposite

---

[154] India Tour

person purely on intuition. A few times, it was the other way round. I met a Bangalore based girl, who was working in WIMC in a different vertical, in Mumbai. She had told me that one of her bad habits was to not respond to alliances if she suddenly felt it was not going to work out. I hoped my fate would not go the same way as the others. We were chatting for a few days but suddenly one day she pinged me saying that she heard rumors about me going around with a HR colleague in WIMC. I replied saying I also heard similar rumors about her. She was surprised. I then told her I was just kidding. She never responded back to messages or calls after that.

3 years had passed and my parents now started to panic. I used to tell this to my friends at work and I would listen to motivational gyaan about "staying invested in the process". Some people also linked arranged marriage to the stock market, stating that patience was the key, and in the long run, the investment would succeed. In between, I also heard a few scary stories about how a few of my friends had been misled by their spouses in the arranged marriage route and harassment cases had been filed in return for money. They had done an out of court monetary settlement and paid a hefty amount and settled for a divorce. I was cursing myself for taking the arranged marriage route.

A friend of mine, who was a self-proclaimed marriage analyst, told me that 3 to 3. 5 years is the average time for a typical GEM (Graduate Engineer Male) to find a girl. He said – "Brother, the arranged marriage market has a huge supply gap; there is a huge shortage of girls. Our previous generations had made a mistake of disproportionately favoring the boy child. As a result, for every 3 males born, you have 1 female. In this skewed scenario, a lot of girls marry their love. The universal set gets further reduced. Amongst the girls who are willing to go for an arranged marriage, people prefer green card holders, boys settled abroad, people with own house and a car, staying independently without parents. On all these factors, you don't score, mate. Mumbai girls prefer someone who wants to settle in Mumbai. South Indian girls prefer someone settled in South. Your XLRI degree is of no use when compared to these factors. Plus, you neither work in a cool startup, nor a foreign-based MNC. So, you will have to wait, as your odds are extremely low."

This was an eye-opener for me. So many factors against me. Had somebody educated me earlier, I would have never gone for an arranged marriage. I cursed the childhood astrologer who had predicted two marriages for me and made me avoid love marriage. It was close to four years now in the marriage search. One of my office colleagues suggested that a senior leader's daughter was looking for a groom and that I speak to him. I rejected the idea. I did not want to create conflicts of interest with the organization later. I waited patiently. In between all this, I had attended a few marriage-meets where I was paraded like a show-piece on the auditorium stage. The only take-aways from these meets were the sumptuous lunch buffets. Nothing clicked.

One day, I received an online profile acceptance request from a doctor from Bangalore. She had kept my profile on hold a few months earlier but now had changed the status to "profile liked". I decided to give it a shot again. We decided to meet in Hyderabad, as she was doing her post-graduation there. I went alone. We met at a coffee shop. She was five feet tall (almost a foot shorter than me in height) but extremely beautiful. I asked her pointedly – "I don't own a house. I don't have a green card.

I am not bothered about horoscopes. I don't know which city I will settle in. I have never been in a relationship. I want us to stay with my parents, post marriage. Will you accept me the way I am and take this forward?" She smiled and asked "Will you let me be the person I am and not force me to make choices which I don't like?" I replied "If your answer to my question is yes, then my answer to your question is yes as well."

After that, we spent a couple of hours chatting on random things and decided to watch a movie. It was one of the worst movies I had ever seen – "Ki and Ka", but it didn't matter as both of us enjoyed each other's company. The girl introduced me to her cousin brother, and that night, the three of us went around the city trying to find midnight dosa[155]. We found an obscure dosa-cart in Nampally, had dosa at 2 am, and I went back to my hotel. The next day, we had breakfast, after which I left for Mumbai. The girl said she needed some time to think and she asked me not to follow up. She said she would get back to me at the earliest. This meeting happened on the 3rd of April 2016. I spent the next few days eagerly praying to God that this would materialize. But I didn't get any response.

Like so many other girls, this one, too, had bitten the dust. I cursed my ill luck. Maybe she had a change of mind. I wanted to follow up with her but since she had specifically told me not to, I did not do it.

A couple of weeks flew by. One day, she called me and said- "Happy birthday in advance, dear. Hope I have made this year's birthday special for you."

[155] South Indian delicacy

16

My Name is Hari & I am not a Terrorist

After a 4 year long wait, I had finally struck gold in my marriage hunt. I felt like giving a "Thank you for the Oscars" speech to all the people who had helped me stay afloat all this while. My wife was originally from Bangalore, pursuing her post-graduation in radiation oncology in Hyderabad. She planned to relocate to Bangalore after the completion of her two-year course. I wanted her to be in the same city as her hometown for the initial years. I had heard from my well-wisher friends that couples in an arranged marriage take a lot more time to settle, and hence, location plays an important role. Therefore, I asked my bosses at WIMC for a transfer to Bangalore. Luckily, they agreed. Being the E. A of the National Sales Head was an advantage for me in this situation as he would himself look for Bangalore based roles for me. My marriage date was fixed for the 6th of November, 2016. As she was based in Hyderabad, every month I would travel down to Hyderabad for the weekend. A lot of my well-wishers told me that the "courtship" period is the best period in a marriage, so it is to be enjoyed the most. The happiness would culminate with the honeymoon, this was the gyaan I received from the experts.

On the work front, as part of the E. A role, I would get to travel to exotic international locations as the CPO (Chief PPT

Officer) for annual dealer conferences. My job would be to man the console in the conference ball room and ensure the PPTs, created by me and others, were played in sequence and everything was integrated logically. After the end of the conference, I would take a day off and explore the location. In the spring of 2016, the dealer conference was in Prague. Prague is till date one of the most beautiful cities I have ever seen. Prague is a mix of both ancient and modern architectures. Prague also was the city where I decided to taste my first alcoholic drink – green absinthe. For someone who hadn't even tasted a beer in his life, the strength of the drink (close to 70% alcohol content) had made me feel that somebody had whacked me on my head. There were four of us and we struggled to finish a single glass. After that, we had no idea what we did. The only thing I remember after that was that I was up in my bed late afternoon the next day.

The next morning, we left for the airport. I will never forget the incident at Prague airport that day. We had finished our security check well before the departure time. I was carrying two bags – one laptop bag and one mini-suitcase as hand luggage. After finishing the security check, we looked for a place to have our breakfast. We walked quite a while but we couldn't find a place. So, we decided to take a break and sit for a while. There was an empty area which had quite a few chairs. All of us sat there. After a while, one of our senior leaders found a place for breakfast and asked all of us to join him. The breakfast was bland to the core. All the items served were ice-cold and hard like stone. We all had no other choice, so we chatted away and had our breakfast. As we had a lot of time left to kill, we spent quite close to an hour at the restaurant.

After a while, I was getting bored. I looked outside through the restaurant window. There were a lot of retail outlets on the opposite side. However, something caught the corner of my eye on the far-right hand side. A bunch of security officials had gathered around the area where we sat a while ago. A few sniffer dogs also were present. The area was being cordoned off. The sniffer dogs were smelling some object and it looked to me like they were trying to detect a bomb. I could not get to see what they were examining. I decided to check this by going a bit closer to the area as we had just sat there moments ago.

When I went closer, I was shocked. The dogs were sniffing my two bags to check for a bomb. I started to sweat now. Initially, I thought I would abandon the two bags, but my office laptop was in one of the bags and there were quite a few important and confidential presentations, whose back-up, I had not taken. I went to the security officials and told them that those were my bags and I had forgotten to take them with me to the restaurant on the opposite side. The officials did not seem to buy this. They asked me to bend down on my knees, with my hands folded on my back, like a convict. I tried explaining them, that I was from a well-known Indian organization and we had come here for a conference. They did not seem to buy my argument. They asked me to surrender my passport. The two dogs came and sniffed me. The fact that I had not shaved and had ruffled hair only added to the doubts in their minds. One of the security officials switched on his walkie-talkie and said "Chief, we have found two unidentified bags in the middle of the airport. An Asian has come saying these are his bags, but we are not convinced. Over." A couple of hefty policemen tonked me on my head. They asked me to keep my mouth shut till they finished checking the bags.

I was asked to call out the items present in the bag. The items would be taken out to verify my side of the story. My bag was emptied out. Out came the filthy underwear bag, a few handkerchiefs, a couple of novels, and my laptops. By this time, quite a few on-lookers had gathered around to see the tamasha. The sniffer dogs sniffed out each and every item which came out of my bag. All the items were scanned through a portable scanner. The senior leader, meanwhile, was trying his best to speak to the officials that this was a case of genuine absent-mindedness from my side and he knew me too well for this to be a terrorist activity. He showed a few selfies he had taken during the conference. Those selfies seemed to give credibility to my story that we were from a well-known Indian company having our conference in Prague, and we had no other business apart from business tourism. Finally, the officials relented after finding that there was nothing fishy, either in me, or my two bags.

All this drama took place in about 20 minutes, but those 20 minutes were the worst 20 minutes of my life. The officials returned my passport to me. While I collected my bags, I overheard the man in the walkie-talkie saying "Chief, we figured this out. The absent-minded idiot had left his bags and gone away. His name is Hari and he's not a terrorist."

17

The Wedding and Beyond

After the fiasco in Prague, it was time for wedding bells in November 2016. It was a typical Indian wedding, but it resembled more of a circus than a wedding. I think "commenting" is the favorite hobby of all the guests invited for a wedding. It started with the mehndi function. At the mehndi function, out came our fashionista aunties with comments like "Arey bahu raani, is lal waali pyjama key saath peeli waali top zyaada achi lagti[156]" These folks should have been guiding Manish Malhotra or Sabyasachi on their latest collection. Some went further, and asked "Bahut sundar dress hai. Kahaan se liya? Kitney mey liya? Thoda mehanga toh nahi hai[157]" As if tumhare jeb sey paise jaa rahe hain... Kapda liya, mehendi ho gaya, tere baap ko kuch nahi hua na... fir kyun daam poochna hai[158]?

Next up, we had a few outstation guests who thought it was their birthright to be treated like royalty. For their personal travel, they would make their own arrangements but when it comes to a wedding, their expectation was that a cab had to be ready waiting for them as soon as they arrived in the city. In case their train arrived early, or the cab driver got delayed, they

[156] The red coloured top would have gone down well with the yellow pyjama

[157] Beautiful dress!!From where did you buy it? How much did you pay for it?

[158] As if you are paying for it. I bought the dress, the mehendi function got over, why bother with the price?

would yell at us with a remark "poor arrangement". In the first place, going out of the way and arranging a cab itself was a big task, as the bride and the groom's family had a zillion things to think of to get a wedding right. But no. That was not their headache. They thought that the groom's family was running a travel agency and any slight deviation such as these would be promptly punished with such snide remarks.

Then, there were the great old men who would think that they knew better than the pandits and would try to contribute their "valuable inputs" regarding the sequence of mantras[159], the timings of various rituals, why "this" event was being added. They would ask us the "rates" charged by the pandits and say, "Don't you think the rates are a bit too high?" Obviously, the rates for a wedding would be high. I wanted to ask these folks "Okay, the rates are high. Would you take their place and do all the rituals on their behalf? Or would you negotiate for a better rate?" The level of commenting was directly proportional to the level of joblessness of these commenting Indians.

A few so-called "busy people" arrived just 15 minutes before the muhurtham[160] (scheduled for 11 am), gave their blessings, and were the first to sit for lunch. These busy-bees gobbled up lunch as if they have not had food in the last 30 days, and left by 1 pm. For them, our wedding was a T20 cricket match. "Jao, shakal dikhao, khana khao aur dafa ho jao[161]." They spent only 2 hours. Rest of their busy time would be spent in reading Filmfare at home to look for news about the next film-star's wedding, putting a wedding check-in on Facebook, taking a few selfies outside, and moving on.

---

159 Prayers

160 Main ritual where the couple ties the knot

161 Go, show your face, eat, and disappear

The stars of the show, though, were the Family Planners. These elders should have become Family Planning consultants with the Government of India. "God bless the child. May you be quickly showered with a little Hari in 6 months' time." I just couldn't understand their obsession with a baby in this already over-populated country of 130 crore individuals. These family planners thought that the couple was a coin-vending machine. Or a McDonald's factory. These Family Planners were more concerned about our next Generation, than about us.

Even more annoying in this set were a few male chauvinist jokers who wished only for a boy baby (why only a boy, why not a girl). They wanted an "Ambi"[162]. I wanted to share my 3-year hunt with them and shout at them for creating the supply shortage of girls in the first place. I would have blasted these idiots with an AK-47(unfortunately, the supply of the rifle is banned, so could not execute this plan). That night, we had decided to stay at a hotel instead of the house as there were relatives around. To that, these jokers gave a wicked smile while giving us a send-off. By the end of the wedding, my poor wife was more relieved than happy as she had seen the back of a bunch of clowns and didn't wish to see them again.

The Family Planners didn't stop their "Nation wants to know" question of when we were going to have a kid anytime soon. They would ask my parents and in-laws about this. "It's been a year and no sign of Junior Hari. When are you giving us the good news?" In every meet-up, the "good news "question would prop up. I don't know what vested interest these folks had in our kid. They behaved as if they would write off their entire fortune in our child's name.

---

162 Ambi in Tamil means little boy.

After 2 years of our marriage, in June 2018, the good news finally arrived. My wife got pregnant and delivered a baby girl in February 2019, much to the dismay of the "Ambi loving" good news brigade. We were overjoyed, as both of us wanted a baby girl for our own reasons. My wife felt that a girl would have a lot more options to "dress up" whereas boys had limited "dressing options" to choose from. For me, it was a selfish myth that a girl child would be closer to a dad than a boy. God had answered both our prayers.

In between all this, I had moved out of WIMC after my wedding and joined AMC (Another Multinational Company) as the Divisional Head for South India. After having spent close to two years, I decided to take a break. I resigned from AMC in January 2019 just a month before my wife's due date. The sales role had a lot of travel and I didn't want to miss out on the most important moment in my personal life. In retrospect, I was glad that I took a break and helped out my wife as it can get very stressful for a lady. After child-birth, I added a few more CV points to my illustrious CV -

"1. Expert in changing diapers. Can change diapers better than 95% of the dad population due to my experience of changing 4 diapers per day.

2. Certification in singing Bollywood songs and putting my baby to sleep. Patented a few songs which are solely reserved for putting her to sleep.

3. Conceptualized and came up with innovative sounds to distract the baby from crying. Some of the innovative sounds include cooing like a cuckoo, braying like a buffalo and mooing like a cow."

At about the same time, I decided to write my first book. I used to draft emails every alternate day in my E. A role at WIMC. I had never thought I would become a writer, but once the thought came into my head, I decided to execute it. I tossed this idea with a few people I knew and they urged me to dream big. My wife suggested that I start blogging as it would help me improve my writing skills. My first blog was about my "30-minute daily bath routine" and it was a huge hit amongst my friends and well-wishers. This motivated me to take writing seriously, and in a span of three months, I finished the first draft of my first book. I decided that the theme for the book would be a funny autobiographical-style satire of me and the events around me. However, I was struggling to end the book.

After my first blog, I started a weekly blog called Freaky Fridays. I completed the first draft of the book in three months, by end of May 2019. However, the manuscript lay in cold storage for a good 3 years, wherein I changed 2 more jobs, before moving to Sheffield in the United Kingdom. After moving to Sheffield in October 2021, I was back on a break again, and this time, I was determined to bring my book to life. From an engineer, to a HR professional, to a Sales Leader, doing the full circle back to HR, and in the process, becoming an accidental writer dad, life has been a crazy journey for me. I haven't had many regrets in my life so far and I hope I will not have many. If you want to know what happens next with me, wait for a few more years until I finish my next memoir. Picture abhi baaki hai, doston[163].

Cheers to Good Times.
Yours truly

[163] The movie is not yet over